IN GOD'S RADIANCE

IN GOD'S RADIANCE

LINDA SABBATH

AMITY HOUSE
AMITY, NEW YORK

Published by Amity House Inc.
16 High Street
Warwick
New York 10990

Library of Congress Catalog Card Number 87-72986

ISBN 0-916349-26-8

Acknowledgements

Biblical quotes from *The Jerusalem Bible*, Double Day & Co. N.Y. 1966—Appendix V, Teilhard de Chardin, *Hymn of the Universe*, Harper and Row, N.Y. 1965, used with permission.

Contents

He has called you out of darkness
into His own wonderful light.
1 Peter 2:9

Introduction

When we are bathed in the radiance of God, we are cleansed, healed, transformed, and instructed, but more than anything else, we are loved with a pure, powerful, unconditional, irresistible Divine Love. We absorb God's love in waves of flames and tides of invisible mist, or drop by drop, in direct proportion to our consent and surrender—and according to his wisdom. Our childish loves, fears, hates, and attachments are burned into cinders and ashes, and a world of boundless beauty and loving joy emerges. The worm becomes a butterfly. By giving up its myopic cocoon-home of oppressive, blind, dark ignorance, it comes forth to soar into heavens of freedom and limitless beauty. Our tenacious self-hate and guilt is exchanged for a new awareness as we, God's masterpieces, find in ourselves a harmony of incredible beauty. Every being reveals the face of Christ; every event has meaning in the divine plan; every moment becomes a glowing jewel in the tapestry of life. As we tread through the garden of paradise on earth, death becomes a longed-for, joy-filled adventure. Our pains and agonies become united with Christ's pains while we wait only for the inevitable fruits of pruning.

Twenty-five years ago when I still knew only hate and fear, in a crisis situation in my personal life I was enveloped and consumed by blinding, golden light for several days. This phenomenon was strong medicine for a severe illness, and few needed it as desperately as I did.

1

This experience led to my becoming a Catholic and then to my founding the Thomas Merton Center for Contemplation in Quebec, Canada,
where the Prayer of Loving Regard was rediscovered and developed.
This book describes the chief prayer practices taught at the Center (some
have been described elsewhere) which free and consecrate the mind,
the body, and the soul from the disfiguration and deformity we all experience at one time or another. We are freed to discover and experience
ourselves "created in the image and likeness of God"—"as partakers of
the divine nature" promised to us in the Scriptures.

Just a few decades ago, our human formation rested in the hands
of the Church; then it moved to academic circles; now it is often in the
hands of television and other media. Abortion, child abuse, pornogra-
phy, drug addiction, teenage suicide and pregnancy, violence against parents and grandparents, and crimes of every sort are increasingly common and are tolerated within families, which are becoming more fragile
and broken. TV and other mass media cannot provide solutions to these
problems; rather, they are part of the problem. I am not indulging in
an exercise in doom and gloom here; I am issuing a rallying call for
the restoration of our divine selves. My plea is that we refuse to settle
for a life of slavery to degradation.

This book is a call to become discoverers, like our forefathers, who
found a new world. We are called to liberation, to the discovery of ourselves as the noblest and most exalted of creatures. The laws of God
and the laws of love are written on every human heart, to be discovered
and nurtured. Christ is not calling us to get out of a sinking lifeboat;
He is calling us to passionate joy, passionate love, and passionate involvement with his entire creation. He only needs our consent. This
book is dedicated to anyone who has sensed an imprisoned glory within, to anyone who seeks to be more loved or to be more loving; to
have more faith, to trust God and his loving kindness more and more.
I do not pretend to be a scholar or a theologian. I wish only to share
a few simple prayer practices that have opened the doors of divine grace
and love to many friends of God, often disheartened, fearful, and full
of doubt and anguish. Rest assured that I shall pray daily for each and
every person who reads these pages.

CHAPTER ONE

The Jewish and Christian Roots
of Contemplation

As I boarded the plane for Israel on my way to three months of studying Jewish and Christian mysticism at its source, my mind teemed with questions. Some I asked of God, others of myself. What was I, a convert, doing as the director of a retreat center for would-be contemplatives, when so many cradle-Catholics are more steeped in the faith, more holy and more credible than I? Why couldn't my husband and I simply enjoy our prayer life, children, and home, without feeling that we must help people open their hearts to the healing love of God? And why, most of all, hadn't I been able to find the answers to my questions in a book, so I wouldn't have to write one myself, but could relax and soak up the sun and the spiritual vitality of this golden Holy Land, unrolling its bronze deserts and bare hills under the wings of my plane?

Since becoming a Christian in my thirties, leaving a broken past of atheism and sadness behind me, I had felt the same unanswered questions hammering my heart—questions that might never be answered in this life. Christ is the Light of the World, the Scriptures say, and so do I, as I look for that light in the world of my own heart, in the darkness of my own understanding. What do these words mean: "Christ is the Light of the World?" If they are only metaphorical, why do we pray for God's radiance to shine upon us? How could a mere metaphor have almost blinded me for days after my conversion, when I was struck by the golden light familiar to so many other Christians, first among them St. Paul, a sinner on the road to Damascus? Why should retreatants at our Thomas Merton Center in Magog see brilliant light during the icon practice we teach there and become transformed by it into people of prayer? Why, too, do so many dying people see light, then die in peace, or return to tell us they are no longer afraid to die? They return to life only with reluctance, because their work is unfinished.

All these questions came together in a single beam, focused on the center of my research project in Jerusalem: Why had scholars persisted in finding the origins of Christian mysticism only in the cool and bloodless dualism of the Hellenistic Greeks when the Old Testament prophets felt the coal of God's fire on their lips, and the people of Israel saw the column of light that was God-among-them in the desert? Surely it was in the living spiritual tradition of Judaism itself that the mystery lay, hidden behind the Veil of the Holy of Holies. That mystery was what I had come to Israel to plunge myself blindly into, as though I were stumbling through smoke, toward the fire, not safely away from it.

God's love affair with the human race began in the person of Abraham, the first Jew. All of us, since then, can only renew that covenant in our hearts and in our lives. Such a commitment as God made to Abraham and we, through Abraham, to God, is no mere theological idea; it is an urgent, felt turning of heart, soul, and mind to light and the source of light, which is the blood of the universe, the brightness in the eyes of Adam when he first awoke and looked into the face of God.

Throughout the history of Judaism this God, whose grandeur rises inconceivably high above and penetrates deep within the bright, spreading edges of the universe, revealed Himself to man in personal, individual moments. Having seen the glory of God in the burning bush, Moses was never the same again, and he reflected what he had seen in his words and in his life. The man touched and purified by mercy [*hesed*] lives that same, active compassion that pours out from the heart of God. His is no merely human benevolence, but a sharing in God's care for creation, for the beings He made in love, and in his image. Morality for the Jews was thus built not on a philosophic idea, but on the rock of God's presence.

As one Hasidic master wrote of this single inspiration for morality and mysticism: "Yet so great is the furnace of love and fire of yearning in his heart for God's name, to cause him delight alone, that nothing else matters and his aim in his entreaties is not for illuminations to shine in his own soul . . . but to illumine the souls of Israel with these illuminations." The love that bound man and God was the same love that held the community of Israel together, gave it one heart, one purpose.

The Jerusalem of today, like the one of Solomon's time, was a monument to that purpose, a reminder that God, who wrote his laws on stone, is also a living presence in the tabernacle of the heart. Here, in the tabernacle of modern Jerusalem, was that living presence in the stones themselves, the stones that almost cried out when Jesus passed by, in the ancient records of Jewish and Christian prayer practice, and in the lives of believers, whatever their faith, who had come to live at the heart of the Holy Land. Scholars seem to agree that the prayer life of the ancient rabbis and their people was rich with mystical practice and a strong sense that God was dwelling among them in the covenantal ark of their souls.

Shekinah in the Scriptures means "the glory of God-dwelling-among-us." According to the biblical scholar J.D. Pentecost, *Shekinah* appears variously in the Old Testament as light, fire, cloud, or some combination of these three, and one of its most important connotations is "shining." [*The Glory of God*, Multomath Press, 1978, p. 51] Not having had the Hebrew experience of God entabernacled among them, or appearing in their midst as a shining cloud, the Greeks used various words and phrases for "the glory of God," sometimes implying radiance [*phos*] and sometimes blessedness [*dox*]. That the Greeks found it necessary to put asunder what the Hebrews experienced as joined together, struck me as significant in view of the dualistic tendencies Christianity took on as the Greek influence grew.

For the Hebrews, *Shekinah* was associated with the glory of the cherubim, the highest of the celestial creatures, who danced between earth and heaven on rungs of light. We will see later in the vision of St. Teresa of Avila that this ladder was never drawn up, but continued to be an open channel between man and God. *Shekinah* appeared to the prophet Ezekiel as light wheeling like a chariot all over heaven, and was continually spoken of by the whole line of prophets, as was the coming of the Messiah, the Son of God.

"The Angel of Jehovah," no common angel, but God shown forth in the Son, is also described as having "*Shekinah*-glory" and, as such, appears throughout the Old Testament. The Holy Spirit, too, has

Shekinah-glory, but is not identified with it. *Shekinah*-glory seems always to be more a function of God than his very identity, which remains veiled in mystery.

Perhaps the earliest scriptural appearance of *Shekinah*-glory, the felt touch of God by his creation, was the flaming sword of the cherubim blocking man's reentry into the lost Garden (Gen. 3:23), in which the first man and woman were visited by the presence of God. *Shekinah*-glory is both light and dark, appearing to Abraham in Genesis 15:12 as a thick, terrifying cloud, after sundown and during sleep. The covenant with the Chosen People is sealed with God present as a smoking furnace, as it is later reaffirmed by the burning bush (Ex. 3) out of which God spoke to Moses.

Throughout the Sinai peninsula midstofa bushes grow, and because it seldom rains in the Sinai, the intense heat can cause these bushes to catch fire and burn to ashes. So burning bushes are not unusual in the Sinai, but ones that talk and give orders *are* unusual. Although Moses had seen burning bushes before, he had never seen one that was not consumed—or that had addressed him with the authority of God. In Exodus 33:16 Moses talks to God as the one dwelling in the bush, *Shekinah*-ing in it, referring specifically to the *Shekinah*-glory, which told him to take the Hebrews home.

Toward the end of Moses's life, he begged God, "Show me Thy Glory" (Ex. 33:18), but God warned him, "No man shall see me and live." To protect Moses, God covered him with his hand, as He had previously veiled his brightness (like devouring fire) with a cloud (Ex. 24:16-17). So that Moses could see Him without being consumed, God showed not his face, but his back. Even this much sight of God made Moses's face shine so that he had to veil it in order not to blind his people. The word for "back" is used by the writer for "shining" and the word *Shekinah* is often used to mean "the shining." [*The Glory of God*, pp. 51 and 53] Once again, the God who was appearing as veiled or clouded was also experienced as light, a paradox that frequently accompanies the phenomenon of *Shekinah*-glory.

Not only great leaders and prophets like Moses and Ezekiel saw visions of light. A tradition existed of "chariotlore" [*ma'asa merkaba*], which gave the devotee an experience much like Ezekiel's and which was later a major source for Pauline mysticism. The teaching explained the way to ascend to the throne of God, and described who should attempt the ascent, how they might be hindered, how protected, and finally, how they should behave in the presence of God. Ezekiel does not reveal what the throne looks like, nor what, if anything, sits upon it. The real concern for this mystical tradition is achieving the purity of heart necessary for the ascent. The experience is not one of probing into the depths of one's own being or voyaging into the void (to speak in modern terms), but of coming before the King of Kings in glory. The mystic drinks in the attributes of God—love, strength, purity, wisdom, holiness, mystery—and returns to reflect these virtues to others. Throughout the centuries that this practice of the *merkaba* mystics has been undertaken, the goal has always been the same—to be transformed into the likeness of God.

The prophet Daniel's words express most perfectly the vision of God sought by the *merkaba* mystics: "The Ancient of Days took His seat. His vesture was like white snow, and the hair of His head was like pure wool. His throne was ablaze with flames. Its wheels were a burning fire. A river of fire was flowing and coming from before Him." Daniel records that he was seized with trembling and that his face grew pale, a mild response when compared to that of the apostles who saw Christ in his glory on Mt. Tabor.

Throughout the Old Testament such instances of God's presence felt as light can be found, but for our purpose here, it is enough to indicate that from the time God first chose his people, he gave himself to them in a palpable communion, a perpetual pentecost of light shadowed by the veil of the material world. (See Appendix I—Ezekiel's vision.)

As is the case with an individual who is caught up in a vision of God and feels himself let down again, once more behaving in an ordinary, selfish, willful human way, so the people of Israel, as the prophet Ezekiel saw them, enjoyed the presence of God in the Temple, then lost that presence through their sins.

The *Shekinah*-glory in the Holy of Holies was so intense, as we learn from 1 Kings, that it was experienced by the priest as darkness, the same sort of darkness that blots out our sight if we stare directly at the sun. One can't help wondering how the High Priest could carry out his duties in the Holy of Holies since he could see nothing, had no windows to give him natural light, and could have no practice sessions. Once a year in the sanctuary was all he was allowed, so he had to get it right the first time. So long as the priest did his work and the people remained faithful, it was understood that *Shekinah*-glory would remain with them in the Temple. Solomon, builder of the Temple, prayed that it would remain forever, but his own sins and those of his people prevented the prayer from being answered.

The *Shekinah*-glory seen by Ezekiel, its departure, and its return to the Tabernacle is the theme of the prophet's book. He records four stages in the departure of this light that had dazzled him in his vision. Each stage is marked by a pause, as if God were waiting to see if his people would repent. First, the *Shekinah*-glory moves out of the Holy of Holies and brightens the whole temple courtyard as it shines from the door of the Temple. When no repentance is forthcoming from the people, the light moves from the temple door to the outer wall, the wall that overlooked the valley of Kedron and the Mount of Olives. Still Israel sins, so the *Shekinah*-glory moves to the Mount of Olives, where rabbinical tradition tells us it waited for three and a half years before departing from Israel entirely.

Seventy years later, when the Jews returned from captivity in Babylon, they rebuilt the Temple, but knew something was missing. In Haggai 2:9 the promise is written that the departed *Shekinah*-glory will some day reappear in a unique way before the Temple is destroyed, as it in fact was, seventy years after the birth of Christ.

My quest was to discover how and why we Christians today pray almost daily in divine office to see this light; how and why many people, in fact, do see this light of glory and are transformed by it. But almost more than that, I wanted to know why so many devout Christians refuse to believe that this light is anything more than a metaphor. Is this the same light people experience in our contemplative prayer practices at the Center, or were they just psychic and optical phenomena? And is sitting at the Eucharist a valid way to experience this light of God's glory? Will this light accomplish the transformation that Paul promised us in 2 Corinthians and 1 Peter?

Jewish tradition, it appears, included both law and prophecy, rite and wisdom—not mere human knowledge, but divine wisdom, grasped as the imminent crashing of God through the roof of the world. By the time of Christ, a strong current of Jewish mystical thought carried from prophetic times the breathless hope for a new creation and a new Passover that would stream together in the messianic wake of the One who was to come, Immanuel, God-with-Us.

As we see in the Book of Isaiah, an apocalyptic mysticism existed within the mainstream of Jewish thought that brightened and quickened the practical piety of the Chosen People. Even in the time when Jerusalem was a rich and blessed place under Solomon's rule, prophets warned, "Woe to the rich," reminding the Jewish people that it was not in the outward world of material prosperity that they would find their happiness and their peace. Jeremiah went further, seeing the ideal man, the perfect Servant of God as one "humiliated, struck by God . . . laden with our sins." Increasingly, then, the Jew who lived his prayer, who would see God in his heart, had to go through the needle's eye of suffering and purification, letting his wealth, desires, and illusions drop away.

By Roman times, a Jewish *gnosis* was centuries old and poured into the widening waters of Christian mysticism until both traditions were "rivers of light." Both, of course, were colored by the whole spectrum of Greek thought, especially that of Alexandrian neo-platonists like Philo. Yet throughout history the Judeo-Christian *gnosis* has been grounded essentially in moment-to-moment life in this world, where man finds himself enfleshed as a part of history at the same time that he is carried in the hands of God. The Creator was not disdainfully remoate from his creation, but present to it in the form of a mysterious light shining from behind a dark cloud, the same column of cloud that led the children of Israel through the desert and dwelled in the Temple's Holy of Holies. Both the darkness and the light, the paradox of God's hiddenness and his blazing presence in the human heart, are present in God's historical dealings with the Jewish people.

The expectation of the Messiah, the hope for that blessed earthquake that would turn the world into heaven, was not only a collective vision of the *Shekinah*-glory to come, but an experience of the individual Jew in which he might catch a glimpse of the glory with the heart's eyes. A fervent few even went out to pray in the desert, to prepare for the coming of God: ". . . to the degree of their preparation, their fidelity to the Torah, their prayer nourished by meditating on God's great deeds in the past, they believed that they might receive at least some rays heralding the coming of the Shekinah, drink some drops of the water of life, which God will lavish on His chosen ones." [Louis Bouyer, *History—Legacy of Judaism*, chapter 1.]

The Essenes were one such group of mystics, but they were by no means alone in their search, nor was their teaching a novelty in Judaism. In the Psalms we read: "In your light, we shall see light. With you is the source of life" (Psalms 36:9). The scrolls of Qumran, written by the Essenes, clearly show that this ancient linking of God's light with the life of man was the basis for Jewish prayer well into the Christian era. From the earliest sacrifices of animals on mountaintops to the temple ritual of historic times, the Jews refined and spiritualized their holocausts until every action became sacred, an act of faith in the goodness of God. The "sacrifice of praise" begun in a literal sacrifice of an animal, went on to become a "sacrifice of the lips," "the word prayed," the word felt in the heart and lived in the moment.

The rise of Christianity had made mysticism suspect to many Jewish teachers, who believed in good faith that they were guarding the integrity of Judaism against dangerous novelties. Like the Counter-Reformation clergy in the sixteenth and seventeenth centuries, many Jews felt that ecstatic forms of prayer might pull up the people from their rootedness in the Jewish faith. Mystical prayer, as well as the wisdom of the Greeks, was thought to be a breeding ground for breakaway movements like Christianity. In time, rite and law became the unchanging rocks on which Jewish devotion stood, and mystical prayer became an underground river, surfacing only in the *gnosis* of the Zohar or the Kabbalah, much as the mystical tradition of the Catholic Church has been submerged since the Reformation, except for the wells of living water rising in contemplative monasteries or in the hearts of solitary seekers.

Matthew's account of the shepherds' visit to the manger describes a "star" which appeared in the East and "went before them until it came and hovered over the place where the young child was and when they saw the star they rejoiced with exceeding great joy" (Matt. 2:9-11). Christians throughout history have taken this Christmas Star quite literally, and scientists have even speculated that it was perhaps a supernova that is known to have flamed in the skies over the eastern hemisphere for several years at that time before burning out. Though we accept the straightforward gospel accounts literally, we may do well to see a deeper significance to this star than is traditionally taught.

The star appeared and disappeared and reportedly actually hovered over the very house in which Jesus lay. Any literal star that would hover over a house would destroy not only Bethlehem, but the entire planet. What, then, was the nature of this "star"? The root meaning of the word *star* is simply "radiance" or "brilliance," the same root as that for the word *glory,* understood by the writers of the Scriptures as *Shekinah*-glory. For the shepherds in Bethlehem and later the Wise Men of the East, the *Shekinah*-glory has returned to Israel.

The Gospel of John talks about the coming of Christ as the coming of a light (John 1:1-14), a visitation by the glory of God in the tradition so familiar to us from the Old Testament accounts. The Greek word for "dwell" used by John when he writes, "And the Word became flesh and dwelled among us" (vs. 14) is not the same word used for "dwell" in the ordinary sense. It is a word borrowed from the Hebrew *skaney,* drawn from the root of the Jewish word *Shekinah,* meaning not just "to dwell among" but "to tabernacle." Thus John seems to be connecting the reappearance of the long-lost *Shekinah*-glory in Israel to the God-man who was now tabernacled in human flesh and in whom the "Glory of God" was beheld.

At the end of Jesus's three-year ministry, when He died on the cross, the veil in the Holy of Holies was torn and darkness fell over the land, both occurrences echoing Ezekiel's vision of the departing of the *Shekinah*-glory from Israel. With the dawn of Resurrection morning, and the angel shining in white raiment by the empty tomb, the *Shekinah*-glory returned in a new form and was seen a last time during the Ascension of Christ into heaven.

Yet another form of the *Shekinah*-glory may appear in the account of Pentecost, when the "Comforter" promised by Jesus came upon the discouraged disciples sitting in an upper room and lit tongues of flame over their heads, filling them with the Holy Spirit. The birthday of the Christian Church, the born-again body of Christ, was accompanied by the visible presence of the *Shekinah*-glory, which is forever alive in both the hearts of believers and the Eucharist.

I have not yet mentioned an important appearance of the *Shekinah*-glory that had special meaning for me as the prototype of the kind of prayer life I was trying to foster at the Center in Canada. Our private name for that place has always been "Mt. Tabor House" and the chapel is named after the Transfiguration. For reasons that will become apparent, I would like to emphasize particularly the moment in the gospels when the *Shekinah*-glory appeared to the three disciples closest to Jesus during his ministry, and was first revealed to them on Mt. Tabor in a burst of light, accompanying the voice of God which said, "This is my beloved Son...hear Him." That same glory lit the Tabernacle of the ancient Hebrews and overcame the three disciples with fear and trembling. Jesus was "transformed before them; and His face did shine as the sun, and His raiment was white as the light. While he yet spake, behold, a bright cloud overshadowed them" [*photeinos* or "bright cloud" is *Shekinah*] [*Jerome*, p. 93] and God spoke from the cloud as He had spoken to Moses and the prophets (Matt. 17:2-5).

Once again, there was the paradoxical reference to a light wrapped in darkness, bright as a cloud when the sun is about to break from behind it. To my mind rose the words of the contemplative poet Catherine de Vinck, who called God that "light to which the sun is shade." So the vision of God must have seemed to the three disciples, and so it was described by the writers of the Old and New Testaments.

Paul, on his way to persecute Christians in Damascus, knew that bright darkness well, for he was stricken into conversion by a radiance that made him blind for three days. He reported to those with him that "they beheld indeed the light but they heard not the words of Him that spake to me" (Acts 22:9). These friends had to lead him by the hand from the place where he had fallen in the road, for as he said, "I could not see for the glory of that light" (Acts 22:11). Later, Paul wrote of his having seen in that moment the same glory of God [*Shekinah*-glory] that had been seen by the prophets, and in 2 Corinthians 4:5-6 he wrote, "It is God who said that light shall shine out of darkness, who shines in our hearts to give the light of the knowledge and the glory of God in the face of Jesus."

Although Paul's Pharisaic background was of great significance, scholars have become more and more convinced that he was heavily influenced by the Essenes who still dwelt in the Damascus vicinity. [J. Danielou, *Etudes* and P. Benoit, *Jerome Biblical Commentary*] Not until he went to Tarsus, his home ground, however, did Paul apparently have the vision he describes in 2 Corinthians 12:2-4: "I knew a Christian man who fourteen years ago (whether in the body or out of it, I do not know—God knows) was caught up as far as the third heaven. And I know that this same man was caught up into Paradise and heard words so secret that human lips may not repeat them."

Such ecstatic journeys frequently appear in Jewish literature, particularly among the *merkaba* mystics, who cannot have been unknown to the spiritually omnivorous St. Paul. He knew, of course, of the seven heavens opened to Levi in a vision and how the angel invited Levi to enter just as the angel at the sixth gate finally admitted the *merkaba* mystic, exhausted after his ordeals. The Aramaic fragment of this testament found among the Dead Sea Scrolls indicates that Paul's visions were not, as has been thought by many scholars, entirely based on Greek, neo-Platonic models, but have their grounding in the Scriptures, tradition, and practice of his own people. The Dead Sea Scrolls have also made clear that John's light mysticism is far more like that of the Essenes in Qumran than that of the Greeks.

The last pieces of what had been a barely detectable mosaic were falling into place. I saw that the great moments in the life of Christ, told in the gospels, like the great moments in the life of each Christian, were brightened by the same *Shekinah*-glory that the Israelites saw from a distance, shining out of the Tabernacle, and whom the prophets saw behind a veil protecting them from sudden death. As Christ was born in the burst of glory that overhung his stable, so we are reborn into new life. As He was transfigured in light upon Mt. Tabor, we are changed in conversion. The cloud that darkened Israel at the Crucifixion also darkens us as our senses go to sleep in death. Then we experience the blazing light of our own resurrection as we follow Christ's. In the perpetual fire of Pentecost, we have the model of our Eucharist; in the blinding light of the Ascension, we have a prefiguring of the beatific vision we ourselves will someday share. Above all, the old, easy, exclusive linking of Christian mysticism with the dualism of the Greek neo-platonists was breaking down in the face of the evidence of a far older and richer Jewish mystical tradition.

CHAPTER TWO

The Call to Contemplation

And the city has no need of the sun or of the moon to shine upon
it, for the glory of God has illumined it, and its lamp is the Lamb.
Rev. 21:22

At the time I first began to learn what contemplation was, I was an atheist
practicing a form of Hindu meditation that was largely psychological,
not requiring any belief system. Thomas Merton's *Ascent To Truth* was
my introduction to Christian Contemplation, though at the time I didn't
even know Merton was a Catholic priest. After I was baptized a Catholic,
Merton became my spiritual director and I became an extension of his
life in the world, visiting Zen Buddhist sessions, Hindu ashrams, Jewish retreats, and sending him notes on what I was learning. With the
total unreality of children, we spoke of building a Mt. Athos in North
America, a center where contemplatives of all faiths could live together
independently, but cross-pollinating each other's practice. Merton was
dissatisfied with his life at the Abbey of Gethsemane because of medical problems and conflicts with his superior; I was dissatisfied with my
academic life at McGill University as a researcher in cross-cultural religious experience. At the time Merton went to Asia on his last journey,
I was about to buy the farm in Magog, Quebec, which later became the
Center bearing his name.

Though we had begun the project as an interfaith experiment, after Merton's death we became entirely committed to Christian contemplation. Increasingly I was aware of the rich mystical tradition of the Church and increasingly also I was disenchanted with the limitations of borrowed Asian practices. The meditation practice of Asians and many Westerners, it became clear to me, was not what the Judeo-Christian tradition has come to call "contemplation." Since the two are so frequently seen as synonomous, it is necessary to say from the outset that contemplation is *not* emptying the mind in order to merge with the void, nor is it dissolving the personality like a drop in the sea of being. It is not detaching the soul from the body so as to achieve some altered state of consciousness, or exploring the depths of one's psyche. The absence of desire or pain is not the goal of contemplation, nor is self-knowledge, higher consciousness, or even a state of godlike goodness.

Some of these goals, common to the meditation movements of our time, may indeed be achieved along the way by the Christian contemplative, but historically, and in what I have experienced of its practice, contemplation in the Christian tradition has a different source, a different method, and a different end from oriental meditation, however much we may learn from the East about natural human longings for prayer.

What, then, do the great teachers of the Church say contemplation is? Richard of St. Victor, in the twelfth century, called it an "attentive synthesis of fragments, penetrating and loving, which attaches the mind to the realities that it is beholding." St. Thomas Aquinas, immolated in prayer at the end of his life, referred to all his theology as "straw," and said contemplation was "a simple gaze on truth." Carmelite theologians added to that phrase the words "under the influence of love." The voices of many saints agree that "Contemplation is an act of knowledge, a simple act that penetrates the truth, without discourse, in a quasi-intensive way." [P. Marie-Eugene, OCD., *I Want to See God*, p. 458] As a child, when St. Teresa was caught running away from home, she told her parents simply, "I want to see God." No contemplative before or since could have put it any more plainly.

What we teach at the Center can be summed up by saying that love, the love of Christ, is the essential beginning and end of contemplation. It is love that moves the mind to gaze on truth, love that simplifies that gaze until the contemplative sees nothing and no one without divine love. Through this love the soul knows with a knowing that gives birth to more love. Not every Christian contemplative loves or knows in the same way or to the same degree, though he or she loves the same God.

We are all as infinitely various as lovers are, and no single expression of our love exhausts our resources as a race. One person gazes on a sunset and is moved to wonder, silence, withdrawal, and a joyful sense of oneness with all creation. A "spiritual experience" that affects us through the senses produces an aesthetic response. We are hit over the head by the beauty of the physical universe and see stars. Perhaps we are of an intellectual cast, seeing beauty in the dance of fact and the finality of figures. A cancer researcher finds a cure for leukemia and dizzied by gladness, he stands still for a moment, wrapped in peace and silence. He touches the pulse of the world; he *is* the pulse.

At the theological level of awareness, however, we not only are the pulse of the world, we know that we are children of God, cocreators with Him in the love that holds body and soul together, the love that Dante wrote "moves the sun and the other stars." It is the goal of contemplative prayer to unite the will and the emotions in an impassioned desire to transcend the sense world while remaining in it and rediscovering it as divine. The self is joined to the eternal and ultimate object of love, whose existence is intuitively perceived by the soul, thus extending the field of consciousness until it includes the supersensual world. The breath of the mystic is love, a movement of the heart seeking to transcend the limits of finite personality by surrendering to the infinite God, to absorb his personality.

In this moment of giving yourself away, life becomes a miracle, and the walls of the jail crumble, leaving us free. That patch of sky once seen in such a limited way widens until it reaches from east to west. We discover the underlying unity of all things, the rhythm of the universe, the love that permeates the created world and gives us life beyond the grave. The contemplation of God, the most rewarding and heroic of all adventures, makes for a life of many colors, not merely a black-and-white film. It is appreciated not by the mind alone but by the senses tasting ecstasy, the spirit drinking love. Only in a process of total change through a complete transformation of body, mind, and spirit into the image of God are we freed to be what we were all made to be—a throbbing, integral part of the mystical mind and body of Christ.

Such transformation proceeds from prayer that is supernatural or "infused" contemplation, as St. Teresa of Avila and St. John of the Cross call it. It is their understanding of contemplation that underlies both the work at the Center and this book.

What do the open eyes and heart of love look at in this form of prayer? Not the revealed truth of the Scriptures, holy and necessary as that is, not the timeless doctrines of the Church, but God himself. This vision of God does not erase the historic symbols and rituals used by the Church over the millenia to reveal transcendent truths to the human mind and to shape a right conscience. Under the silver surfaces of dogma, St. John of the Cross tells us, lies the gold of divine truth for those who believe. Only the wide-open eyes of faith see that gold, that mysterious life and presence of God. The blind eyes of our intellect close so that the heart and soul can see.

As the intellect is "darkened" or diminished, a confused light, an "I-know-not-what," as St. John of the Cross says, arises through the Holy Spirit and touches us first with peace, then with gentleness, then widens to brighten the whole sea of faith, freeing us from the neat schemas of the finite, left-brained intellect. Our poor, tired minds find rest and joy and leap like men on the moon in this light of lights to which "the sun is shade."

More than a metaphor, this light is *Shekinah*-glory, the source of that love and knowledge we have become. In *The Ascent of Mount Carmel*, John of the Cross says: "These lofty manifestations of knowledge can only come to the soul that attains to union with God, for they are themselves that union, and to receive them is equivalent to a certain contact with the Divinity, which the soul experiences, and it is God Himself who is perceived and tasted."

The many hundreds whom I have seen learn to practice contemplative prayer at the Center testify that the Holy Spirit is eager to give us this grace for the asking, so long as our commitment to Christ is pure and honest. These witnesses, like Christ himself, tell us to "Taste and see."

Love not only strips the dark veil of ego from the soul, it gives birth to more love, more knowledge. This supernatural love, from God, of God, and for God, multiplies like loaves and fishes into care for creatures, for man, for God-the-Maker. Contemplation is "the science of love," which unites God's love and his will. Only one thing did St. Teresa and St. John ask of their wordless communion with God: that it might lead to perfect union with Him, with eyes that see the same sights, hands that bless the same broken bodies, love that knits the creation into one God-shaped form. Love has no other end than to go on loving, and our prayer is only one small open door through which love comes in full dress, with flutes, drums, and blazing lights, a bright parade into that dark city of ourselves, lit dimly by the fireflies of art, the candles of intellect.

Even the mysteries of scriptural events are no more than blinks in the light of revealed truth. Supernatural contemplation penetrates to divine truth, to God himself, the uncreated Light, the Sun with burning, healing rays, that is not consumed. In this fire of the infinite God, in this burning bush, we die to our false self and are born again. In supernatural contemplation, the soul, like a crystal refracting a billion rainbows when held up to the sun, like the log thrown into a fire, is transformed into the energy of light and heat by the all-consuming God.

The comparisons found in the lyricism of St. John of the Cross and other mystics recount the steps of the soul as it walks into intimate union, hand-locked with God in contemplative prayer. By the alchemy of love, the soul is purified, illumined, dressed in light, beauty, and the riches of God, wearing Him like a wedding garment. St. John of the Cross writes: "This is an infused and loving knowledge of God, which enlightens the soul and at the same time enkindles it with love, until it is raised up step by step, even unto God, its creator." Transformation in God is the single end toward which the truly contemplative soul tends, committed to the road of Nothing on its way to Everything.

My own road to the Absolute, which I have been traveling for many years now, has physically ended at the Center, a 140-acre farm situated twelve miles north of the Vermont border (but on no map—as true places never are). The beautiful mountain range in the distance, the "Delectable Mountains," as one retreatant called them, in the spirit of her own *Pilgrim's Progress*, recall the words of the Psalmist: "I will lift up my eyes unto the hills, from whence cometh my help." Help was exactly what I needed when I arrived there with three children, an uncertain future, and no money. My call to contemplation was no crazier than anyone else's, but at the time it seemed crazy enough to make my friends shake their heads.

The house, or rather the remains of a house, had been previously inhabited by animals and a mentally retarded family. It was evaluated at $100 and, according to the architect, fit only for burning down. The barn was in better shape, and the whole place had undeniable features for the project Merton and I had envisioned. The property was across the lake from the Benedictine monastery of St. Benoit-du-Lac, and when the wind was right, their bells could be heard early in the morning. A new school for the children was opening up, and although it was forty miles away, there was a door-to-door bus service. That first summer, a number of enthusiastic priests from Montreal arrived to shovel the manure out of the house, to paint, scrub, and help remove six truckloads of garbage, some of it dating back 150 years. Food had to be cooked outside except on rainy days when we struggled with a one-burner hotplate. Donations of old furniture started to arrive, enthusiasm ran high, and the old orchard started to ripen. The first renovation was the bathroom plumbing, hooking it up to the cesspool instead of letting it drain into the basement, and by the end of the summer, the mysterious network of water pipes had been repaired and was producing drinkable spring water. In late August, the first retreat was given by a Tibetan Buddhist monk, but only one Mass had been celebrated as yet, chiefly because the priests did not consider it appropriate.

At the beginning of September, everyone returned to the city except me and my three children. A car accident demolished my car and left me immobilized with neck and back injuries. My child support was withdrawn, forcing me to go on welfare and to ponder the wisdom of my move. Like all hopeful contemplatives, I tried to search for God's will in the matter, sure that He would pick me up, even if I fell flat on my face.

The children were delighted: the new school delayed its opening until Christmas, there was no functioning bathtub, and someone gave each of them a brand-new colt from a nearby farm. As winter approached, the uninsulated frame house grew colder, ice appeared on the inside walls, and we had to sleep in arctic ski-doo suits, covering ourselves with paper and plastic. A hundred-pound bag of cracked wheat was our mainstay, with occasional rancid meat bought "for the dog," and covered in curry. At times there was more mail than food. People wrote from different parts of North America, Hawaii, and Switzerland, asking to join the community or to visit. Sometimes mail was not answered for weeks, if the choice was between stamps and bread.

When Teresa of Avila was a young nun of twenty, her uncle gave her a book on prayer, a classic of the period entitled *The Third Spiritual*

Alphabet, by Francisco de Osuna. This book was Teresa's sole guide to prayer for twenty years, and the saint's copy, heavily underlined, can be seen in St. Joseph's Monastery in Avila. Osuna began his book by stating: "Communion with God may be attained in this life by all."

We are all called to contemplation; nobody is left out. Priests and nuns can't do it for us, nor can paid Masses, nor helpful saints. Speaking not only of the call to the mystical life, but explicitly of the call to contemplation, St. Teresa wrote:

> Remember, the Lord invites us all and, since He is Truth Itself, we cannot doubt Him. If His invitation were not a general one, He would not have said: "I will give you to drink." He might have said: "Come all of you, for after all you will lose nothing by coming; and I will give drink to those whom I think fit for it." But, as He said we were all to come, without making this condition, I feel sure that none will fail to receive this living water unless they cannot keep to the path.
>
> *The Way of Perfection*, XIX, Peers 11, 85

At the beginning of the next chapter, the Saint reminds her readers that whichever way souls find God, going by the active or passive paths, they must be brave. This fight is to the death.

Make no mistake, the Saint's books assured me, shivering in my ski-doo suit; you are in a war, whether you like it or not. You have to be on fire. You have to be willing to die rather than fail to listen to God in prayer. "What other choice is there?" I whispered to myself as the snow closed over our little farm like a heavy white hand. "There's no other way to go." The winter grew colder, food scarcer, and the water pipes froze. Even food on the kitchen counter froze and had to be refrigerated to keep it soft enough to eat. Just as St. Teresa had understood the human situation long ago, so I understood it now, my fingers blue in the wind of the Canadian winter, but hanging on. "Not only saints," I said to myself under the covers, "but sinners, too, are called. Christ's arms are full of broken bodies, broken hearts." The thought warmed me and I slept, long and often, until the sun came back in the spring.

One holiness, one healing, is all there can be, but the one body that is healed has as many members as a winter storm has snowflakes. Each touches God and the others in love, however various the roads that lead to the mountaintop from remote points on the map of the human soul. As roads wind, drop, and rise, so do we. Our spiritual gifts are as individual as our noses. God works in unpredictable ways in our souls. In the dark laboratory of our wisdom, we cannot see where his hands reach or what strings they touch. Our poor brains cannot discover truth, no matter what scientific instruments are at hand. In us echoes what millenia of saints and sages have told us from their hearts and what we must receive with the alert antennae of our hearts.

And what do they say, these antennae of the spirit? St. Teresa wrote that there are many roads to God, as there are many mansions in heaven. It is possible, she suggested, that some souls on the path do not have the joys of contemplation. Though they may not advance here on earth, where their feet are stuck in ordinary soil, their faith and love will draw them into the arms of God as surely as air is drawn to lungs and light to moons. Any spiritual director knows that St. Teresa is right about the straight path to God, where no one can miss a step, even while dancing.

If, however, you hear the call of God, answer; never mind whether it is general, proximate, or hard to hear. If you experience hunger and thirst for God, you are called to love Him. The call shakes in you like the clapper on a bell and you know whose music is being played. You sing in answer, dancing in the rain, wet with the water of life. "So," wrote St. Teresa, "do not tarry on the way, but strive like strong men until you die in the attempt, for you are here for nothing else than to strive. . .always pursue this determination to die rather than to fail to reach the end of the road."

By the end of that first winter on the farm, I knew what St. Teresa meant by the strength of strong men, and so did my children. In the spring we came out of that drafty, broken-down house, hard as tree trunks. cheerful as daffodils, ready for anything. Soon two men came from Madonna House, bringing cheer, hope, liturgy, and the Divine Office, and began planning the spring garden, for the snowdrifts were disappearing. All of us prayed for God to send the Center a wealthy, saintly priest who was also a competent plumber, electrician, musician, farmer, and lover of noisy children. A Carthusian monk arrived from Switzerland barely speaking English or French, but celebrating Mass daily. He dreamed our dreams with us, and others came with the spring and summer.

Peter—who later became my husband—arrived that summer, having had his fill of universities and travel. His only desire was union with God, which he articulated as "enlightenment." He took over the sheep-raising, the gardening, and the reparation of endless broken windows and walls. He tried to figure out why Mass was so intensely appealing to him, why he dreamed of becoming a priest and what to say to his agnostic Jewish parents when he became a monk. He moved rapidly into becoming a totally committed Christian, comfortable with all the Christian mystics and saints. He became less comfortable with psychological systems, with Asiatic religions, and—at last—became a founding father of the Center.

In the early years, many retreatants who came to us were afraid of the word *contemplation*, even though they might have unknowingly practiced it for years. Their modesty and misinformation presented a problem for us. Was it the same thing to be called as to be chosen? Surely, if Peter and I had been able to practice contemplation without even knowing the Hail Mary, other Christians would have no trouble learning to pray contemplatively. During one retreat, we tried to slip in a bit of contemplation by calling it "the prayer of listening," much like a mother sneaks vitamins into her child's orange juice. It always worked. People who were certain that contemplation was too exalted for them were thus able to practice it and receive from it the graces they needed to digest the fruits of prayer in their everyday lives.

We have observed that fewer professed religious are telling us that contemplation is presumptuous and only for saints, and an increasing number of lay people are aware that *The Living Flame of Love*, St. John of the Cross's greatest and last work, was written for a laywoman in Spain. The charismatic movement has taught increasing numbers of religious and laity that a variety of powerful religious experiences are possible for ordinary Christians. The new and intense spirituality being enjoyed in Christian churches requires new vessels, new forms of worship and spiritual expression, for the old ones are bursting from the new wave of contemplation.

Because spiritual experience is no longer a rare wine affordable only by the happy few, we find we can straightforwardly use words like *mystical* or *contemplation* and works like St. John's and St. Teresa's without alarming anyone. Still, we are very careful in teaching the central practice of this chapter—the prayer of loving regard or icon-gazing. For centuries, it was thought that this practice could be dangerous to a person's sanity, and we, too, were concerned that not everyone was ready for it.

We studied Jewish and Christian spiritual masters to learn how they had dealt with the effects of concentration of this kind. They taught us that it is a great risk for those unprepared and uncommitted to God. For years, we have recommended that our retreatants not explain or discuss this practice outside the Center. Until recently, we have also refused to write about it or disseminate information about it. Now, after fifteen years of experience, we are satisfied that no harm has come to anyone who has a heartfelt desire to follow Christ and who lives by the teachings of the gospels and the authority of the Church. Even skeptics and nonbelievers have been transformed by the prayer of loving regard into devout, enthusiastic, and loving Christians, while a careless, sensation-seeker can experience what Teresa of Avila called "stupor" and remain in this condition for years.

When I was a child of seven or eight, bored to death in the classroom, I discovered that by fixing my eyes on the shiny corner of the desk, I could make everything around me disappear from view and sit in a sort of cloud of peace. Although I am not sure what this practice contributed to my life, I know that it was around this time that I began to ponder infinity. Much later I found that the philospher Emmanuel Kant used a similar method to attain mental lucidity by narrowing and simplifying the conscious field when he "found that he could better engage in philosophical thought while *gazing steadily* at a neighboring church steeple." [Evelyn Underhill, *Mysticism*, p. 50]

This is not to say that contemplation of God is easy, simiple, or "natural"; only that the capacity for it is built into every human being, as are heart, lungs, and vocal cords. Somewhere out of the depths of my yearning for God, out of my pains, my ecstasies and raptures, out of my dreams and my abandonment to God, I knew that I knew that I had been told how to cultivate contemplation through specific prayer practice.

At the age of sixty-two, when St. Teresa set to work on *The Interior Castle*, she was aware of the egotistical motives that can invade the spiritual life. She had been ordered by her director to write the account of her spiritual development, but she felt she had no more to say than she had said already. Too many ecstatic mystics had said too much. Had she not already written *The Way of Perfection* (1562) and *Exclamations of the Soul to God* (1566 to 1569)? Was she not still engaged in writing the *Treatise on the Visitation of Convents* (1576)? What more could she say? As she wrote in her prologue to *The Interior Castle*, "I'm afraid I'll repeat myself, like the birds." Because then, as now, contemplation meant obedience, St. Teresa began to write what she had seen of God's dealings with her. She saw a crystal globe, a castle, in which God, the King of Glory, lived. The closer one drew to Him, the brighter was his light. Outside the castle, toads and vipers dwelled. The stench of filth filled the air. But, inside, light beamed.

At the Center, we asked an artist to draw Teresa's vision for us, similar to what Bernini did for the Vatican. He painted a bright golden center, surrounded by concentric circles representing seven mansions, each circle becoming progressively dimmer the further it was from the center, which represented the Trinity. A simplified form of this "icon" is used at our retreats as an aid to focussing the attention. Because the seven circles proved distracting to beginners in this form of prayer, we placed one small, gold circle in the middle of a brown square, before their eyes. Early examples in Christian art of such a bright circle drew the eye into a reality beyond the physical. Throughout the history of religious iconography, similar circles of light had surrounded the heads of Christ or his saints. By the time of St. Teresa, it was common for disks of light to surround the heads of holy people, and it is no surprise that the just soul appeared to her in a vision as a clear diamond with a brilliant light at the center of brightening concentric circles of light. Each separate zone constituted a separate mansion, much as each cell of the body contains a subatomic universe. The vision, however, is no more than a symbol, in comparison with the luminous splendor that shone out from it and showed St. Teresa what to say about the castle: "which is nothing else than a paradise where Our Lord, as He says, takes his delight" [*Mansions I*, Peers II, p. 201] How might she speak of the in-nermost mansion of this circle, a place both dark and mysterious? [*XVI Mansions I*, Peers II, p. 230, *V Mansions I*, Peers II, p. 247, VII p. 239]

God answered her prayer, gracing her with the very effects she would describe. She was seen as the people of Israel saw Moses, her face shining as she transcribed the Word of God. [Note: *The Interior Castle*, Peers II, p. 196] St. Teresa's dynamic vision reflected the old Judeo-Christian prayer practice that was present in so many forms in the Spain of her time. The *merkaba* mystics gazed on circular pools of water or on polished bronzed mirrors to concentrate their attention, and the similarity to the practice of St. Teresa has been noted by scholars.

Not only is it very possible that Teresa was exposed to the mysticism of Christian Kabbalism, but it is difficult to imagine how she could have avoided it, given the times she lived in. Christian awareness of the Kabbalah was already strong in Spain when Teresa was born there in 1515. One of the richest empires in the world at the time, Spain had been highly developed in intellectual-mystical circles for about 250 years before Teresa's birth. There is every likelihood her Jewish grandfather was well aware of it from both Jewish and Christian sources. Even more likely was Teresa's knowledge of Jewish mysticism through the Florentine school of Christian Kabbalah founded by Picodella Mirandola (1463-94), whose works were translated into Latin, stimulating writings in Germany and France as well as study by cardinals and priests alike.

Daily, in our Chapel of the Transfiguration, we looked upon icons of transfiguration, showing the apostles falling over, overwhelmed by their vision of Christ's glory. Such images are:

> drawn from the material world to transmit the revelation of the Divine World, making this world accessible to understanding and contemplation. Flesh is transfigured, radiant with divine light, and is not a representation of the Deity, but an indication of the participation of a given person in Divine life. It is a testimony of the concrete, practical knowledge of the sanctification of the human body...a guide...on the way toward transfiguration.)
>   [Ouspensky, *The Meaning of the Icon*, pp. 5-8]

Daily we gazed upon the Eucharist in the monstrance at evening adoration, not yet fully aware of the excesses of and resistances to this joyful prayer, only aware that we were gazing at glory and that this glory was transforming us.

With the history of the icon in mind, we put our little one to work at the Center, placing it before the gaze of all kinds of people. We told them they were practicing what we then called "the prayer of listening," but which has gone by other names—"icon-gazing," "the prayer of loving regard," "the prayer of quiet," or, in the langue of St. Teresa, "the prayer of Simple Union." None of these terms completely describes the whole process of this form of prayer, nor all its effects.

The practice may begin in recollection, turn to the prayer of listening, and very soon become adoration, even union. During the practice, some may hear a whistle-like wind in their ears, and others may smell a sweet fragrance. Still others see light or moving figures. All of this and more can happen within the half-hour time we allot for the practice. Much depends on the person's spiritual needs, the specific grace being prayed for, which theological doubt needs resolving, or which insight a person requires in the way of purification and healing—whatever God knows is the greatest need. Because the range of need and effects is so broad, we have finally settled on calling icon-practice the "prayer of loving regard," reminding those who practice it that they are not to become sleepwalkers or puppets, but are to remain alert, in constant vigilance against distractions, daydreaming, or the incursion of diabolic influences.

We are always happy to hear people ask if this practice is "quietism," for every precaution must be taken against turning over one's mind and soul to any bizarre recommendation that comes along. Many Catholics who are overdeveloped in the purely rational mode, yet who crave a direct experience of God in their innermost being, sometimes find themselves investigating, even practicing, primitive forms of spiritism, psychism, and other dangerous forms of occult practices that further impede their experience of God's love.

Quietism has a long history in the Church, beginnnning with the earliest centuries, and was first condemned in 383 A.D. For the quietist, only prayer mattered; sacraments and good works were unnecessary, for the soul was already freed from evil desires and actions by its prayer. The medieval quietist went so far as to say that perfection can be obtained in this life, and that once "perfect," the person can ignore the laws of church and state. They taught nonresistance to desires of the body, indulging freely in sexuality, making no effort to grow in virtue.

The error of the quietists was not in surrendering to God through contemplative prayer, but in mistaking their own will for God's and acknowledging no carryover between the experience of God in prayer and the doing of his will in everyday life. Their morality was somewhat like that of today's "me generation" as it does its "own thing." The second-rate psychologies that espouse such "morality" have shadowed even the moral life of the contemporary Church. For this reason, every care must be taken to bring back contemplative practices into the post-Vatican II

Church with the safeguard of rigorous obedience to divine and human law, as well as the guidance of a sound director, if at all possible. A director should, ideally, be a saint who remembers being a sinner. Since few such guides are available, one may have to rely on a supportive Christian prayer group, whose members are available to counsel each other "in the Spirit," and which has access to the help of a wise, holy, and well-trained religious teacher when help is especially needed. The important thing to remember is that no one is more subject to delusions of pride and grandeur than the solitary soul, intoxicated with the joy of "seeing God." Like anyone who has had "too good" a time at a party, such a soul may well need to be helped home by a sober friend.

Most of what has been written in this chapter so far has been to prepare the reader for the prayer practice of loving regard. This kind of practice has traditionally been reserved for the very brave, for the pure in heart, for spiritually and physically mature persons, and for persons with a support group. Even with all of those qualifications, a person might still become frightened and flee. For that reason, also, we keep a large painting of the Transfiguration in our chapel, showing how the apostles were frightened when they saw Christ transfigured on Mt. Tabor.

Early in the Center's history, we emphasized gazing directly on the Eucharist in a simple monstrance. Some contemporary theologians, however, wanting to avoid certain excesses, discourage gazing upon the Eucharist in this way. In fact, we were told at a retreat we gave in Louisiana that it was specifically forbidden in some of the dioceses in the United States. There is wisdom in this prohibition, for our goal is to be in touch with the indwelling Holy Spirit, not so much any external thing, even God.

One last preliminary note may be useful before a person begins this powerful practice. The *kataphatic* prayer that is familiar to Catholics emphasizes images, symbols, sensations, and vocal prayer. The rosary is one example. *Kataphatic* prayer, like any other form, has its hazards: over-attachment to sensation and feelings. The *apophatic* type of spirituality taught at the Center is beyond words, images, feelings (except for the love of God), and sensations. It is dangerous only if it becomes the person's exclusive form of Christian practice, throwing his or her life off balance. In such cases, it can become antiincarnational, leading to disrespect for the body's need for movement and work in the world.

It can lead to self-centeredness and pride, to a sort of stupor that hinders one from showing active love for others, as well as to endorphine highs which may look like divine ecstasy, but are, in fact, purely natural physiological reactions to sensory deprivation.

With all these warnings in mind, we begin our prayer of loving regard in our chapel, having offered our prayer to God and acknowledged the presence of the Blessed Sacrament. If a chapel is not available, we suggest finding a quiet corner and seating yourself comfortably, with the icon taped to the wall at eye level. Read aloud a passage from the Scriptures that mentions light, such as this one:

> But we all, with unveiled face beholding as in a mirror the glory
> of the Lord, are being transfomred into the same image from glory
> to glory; this is the work of the Lord who is Spirit.
>
> 2 Cor. 17-18

Next, take the three steps mentioned by St. Teresa before beginning any prayer: place yourself in the presence of God, sign yourself with the Cross of Christ, and examine your conscience in the light of the Holy Spirit.

An important preliminary to the prayer of loving regard is the Examination of Conscience (a complete text of the Examen we use is in the Appendix), or Consciousness, as it is often called now. By making the examens an "exercise of awareness," many Jesuits are hoping to make it not merely a catalog of good and bad actions, but a total survey of the place of God in one's daily life. St. Ignatius Loyola laid down the format for this exercise 400 years ago and no one has been able to improve on it since.

> 1. We begin the exercise with thanks to God and an acknowledgment that we owe him all we have, all we are.
> 2. Only He can give the light of the Spirit for which we now pray and show us insights into our own mystery. We ask for help in seeing the gifts of God in the day's events and ask that we will be shown by the Spirit where in our lives we are not responding to the love of God.
> 3. A survey of the past day follows, in which we allow the important moments of choice and challenge to pop up in our consciousness like corks on the surface of the sea. How might Christ have

been trying to draw you to himself during this day? In what events, what people, did you encounter Him?

4. Contrition/sorrow: As Christ's presence grows more radiant for us, we see ourselves honestly, realizing how far we are from being Images of God.

5. Resolution and hope: May I be attentive to God's presence around and in me; may I be able to discern, with God's help, the ways in which he is trying to touch me, draw me, and love me during these moments I am about to spend in his presence.

As many as possible of the above preliminaries should be carried out before you or your group actually begins the thirty minutes of the prayer of loving regard with the icon. To ease your mind and body, which may be tense with anxiety or expectation, breathe deeply and regularly. Sit straight but not stiffly, your hands relaxed in your lap. Gaze into and beyond the icon with no thoughts, no words, no images. A headache may result if the eyes and mind are searching for signs, wonders, or anything at all. So just cultivate a relaxed, simple gaze, as if you were observing a sunset or a pool of water. Silently be present in the moment with the indwelling Holy Trinity. As the Orthodox liturgy says, "Be attentive! Be attentive!"

What reactions may be experienced to this icon-gazing, this prayer of loving regard? For some people, the experience will simply be one of peace and "recollection" (in the sense of "pulling oneself together"). For others, it may be the sight of images from the unconscious, flickering light, the sensation that one is being drawn into a bright tunnel, or that the icon explodes in light. To still others, the icon practice is a direct road to supernatural contemplation, in which case the icon and all other images drop away, forgotten. (Note: At the beginning, it may be a good idea to practice for only five minutes, working up gradually to the thirty-minute limit.)

In our experience at the Center, a few people find the practice unappealing and even frightening. Black despair may overcome them; the time may crawl unbearably; ugly images may frighten them. For such people further cleansing and healing are necessary. One such person was a twenty-five-year-old nun who had been raped as a child, and who had not yet been helped to a healing of this trauma. We read from the nun's journal:

> A very ugly picture of a man and woman kissing each other with
> rotten teeth falling out of their mouths, rotten eyes falling out, a
> decaying face with worms crawling about, clumps of dirty hair fall-
> ing out of their heads. Tried it three times. Same every time.

Such an experience clearly shows that the practice should be dis-
continued at once, and healing be sought. We referred this nun to thera-
py, but sometimes a healing of memories session will accomplish the
necessary cleansing. Directors and practitioners both should keep careful track of what images appear and persist during this prayer of loving
regard, especially if they are negative ones.

To forestall such problems, we run a three-minute test before the
icon for our retreatants to see if they are ready for the practice, following it up with a five-minute test to be quite sure the retreatants can handle it. With the exception of a few who had been burned out on drugs,
who were psychotic, or who had in their hearts an unresolved moral
problem, we had positive responses. The usual answer was that the icon-
gazing had been pleasant, that the time had passed quickly, and that
a neon-like flickering of light altered the appearance of the icon. Probably the high percentage of strong, positive reaction would not be near-
ly so great outside the Center or some other place where deeply committed people are gathered in prayer.

Even these positive experiences may be received in a negative way
if obstacles such as doubt or fear are present. Take the case of a sixty-
five-year-old engineer describing his resistance to the prayer of active
attention:

> I can't do this kind of thing, which looks like nonsense. I feel silly;
> it can't be prayer. . .I wish I could leave right now. . .[Later]. . .I
> saw a blue light which must be an optical illusion and I spent the
> whole time trying to discover the source. Then it escaped me and
> it did not return. The blue light is present and so is great calm and
> wonder. It is becoming appealing.

Doubt is a considerable obstacle at the beginning of this practice.
So is that initial absence of "*kataphatic* props" which give us that familiar
feeling of prayer that we are used to from childhood. The prayer of lov-

ing regard may be blocked by a feeling of excessive strain and effort; of fear at what may happen; of boredom; of resentment; of impatience. These feelings are nothing but brief surges of emotion having no more effect on will, faith, and love than does the wind blowing over water.

Directors or advisors to prayer groups should be aware, however, that where a person is not prepared by faith, discipline, and holy living, a dropping of the barriers in *apophatic* prayer can release a surprising flood of purgative material which may even appear demonic until brought into the divine light for restructuring. On the other hand, the break in the dike of the conscious mind can also admit the onrushing tide of love and light in which God bathes his universe and his people, but which we cannot see with bodily eyes. Characteristic responses to the prayer of loving regard show a sense of closeness, of being loved, and of being at peace. The barriers seem to drop away between the ego and the unseen spiritual world. Several representative accounts follow:

From a forty-five-year-old Sister Provincial:

> For the first time since I entered my order, I have felt the closeness to God that I have been craving since adolescence. It was the same kind of closeness that I had with God when I was a little child on the farm. What peace, what relief, that I know how to regain those glorious moments.

From the journal of a fifty-year-old laywoman:

> At first I was anxious, and felt strained in my back, but the second time I was relaxed and felt such an inflowing of love as I have never felt before. I knew it was God's love, and I felt like the most loved person in the whole world, ever. It has continued every time I did this prayer for this week, though not always as strong as the first time.

Like many other retreatants (see the Appendix for more complete accounts), these two saw bright, neon-type light flickering at the edges of the icon, which appeared to pulsate. Some see a violet or blue ring around the border or across the surface. Those who continue in this practice till the end of the retreat (about 75 percent of those who come to us) get closer and closer to that brilliant center, the Holy Trinity, that

St. Teresa saw in her vision. Generally, the further away a person is
from experiencing the indwelling Trinity, the dimmer the light. The closer
the person is, the brighter the light.

Very often people experience the practice as a transforming union,
but are unable to return to it either because they lack a director or because they lack understanding of what grace to ask for. Such people have
no idea how to prepare for a grace or how to retain it once it is given.
The charismatic "baptism in the Holy Spirit," for instance, can be an
entry into the prayer of loving regard, but a follow-up is needed which
will help the person translate his or her prayer into loving action. We
should make clear at this point that the three classic stages of prayer—
purgation, illumination, and union—do not follow each other in a cut-
and-dried sequence. Though we dwell mainly in one mansion, we visit
the others on occasion. You may, for instance, need a great deal of cleansing, as did St. Teresa, yet be granted an isolated experience of "union"
with God. God does not follow any rule except that of love. Whatever
is in our best interest, He can be depended on to give us.

Frequently we have found in our practice at the Center that God
instructs us in images from deep in our own consciousness. Our eyes
are not constructed to see them ordinarily any more than we can see
the dimensions of a nuclear field, the structure of atoms, or the elec-
tricity that flows through copper wiring. Our ability to sense reality is
very limited. The deer of the forest far surpass our human capacity in
their keenness of smell. Bats possess a phenomenally sensitive built-in
radar system. Some animals can see things in the dark that escape our
attention. Swallows, geese, and salmon possess sophisticated guidance
systems that appear to border on the supernatural. So why should we
think it strange if we fail to perceive the evidence of God's glory or other
divine presence? Still, we must be careful not to let ourselves be carried away by these constructs of the imagination.

Some images can destroy contemplative prayer if not rejected immediately. One such image persistenly stayed with a priest on his second week of retreat, after he had made rapid progress during the first
week. Having seen symbols of purification (bathrooms) and of illumination (tunnels and doors), he began to see a North American Indian
in profile. This image continued for several sittings for three days. It
was completely out of character and I was unable to see any kind of
possible meaning. Just as I was about to ask him to discontinue the prac-

tice, he received a card from a close friend with this same Indian head on it.

Such a parapsychological experience would have been harmless had the priest not become so captivated with thought transference and other esoteric matters that his prayer life suffered. When he finally realized that he was becoming more and more alienated from God, losing his sense of joy and union, he gave up the practice and returned to the avenues that took him closer to God.

Images seen during the prayer of loving regard can also seduce the mind into manipulating dream material. Some people are even able to pick up the same dream from night to night and go wherever it takes them. Or one may habitually be drawn into dream material from an earlier time in which unresolved conflicts still lie. These dream images are not a hindrance, except if one cultivates them in prayer. Of course they may turn up involuntarily, even while a person is partially praying. Occasionally we find a person is able to sleep very lightly while doing this practice, and appear to be deeply engaged in prayer, complete with "consolations," opening the door for Satan. If one is not alert and attentive to the *purpose* of the practice, i.e., union with God, other influences can creep in past one's dropped guard.

St. John of the Cross warns us to learn from these images, but not to make a career out of them. In chapter sixteen of *The Ascent of Mt. Carmel*, John speaks of images as "imaginative visions," that is, pictures from sources other than the senses alone—from memory or fantasy. For this reason, we should be careful not to rely too much upon them. As soon as a person becomes attached to a vision, or even concentrates upon it for temporary enjoyment and instruction, the vision becomes an impediment, even a danger. Because they may come from God or be vital messages from deep in our own unconsciousness, however, we should pay respectful attention to them. In modern terms, images are the intuitive, right brain's way of dealing nonconceptually with the complex religious experience of call, conversion, and cleansing, each of which involves the pain of self-knowledge, the struggle to make right moral choices, and the strain of learning to put God's will ahead of one's own.

The most common images reported by our retreatants are clouds, fire, birds, and mountains. The Scriptures recount God's appearance in such forms as clouds, fire, or on a mountaintop. In the universal iconography of the human race, the bird represents the human soul, and specifically in Christianity, it represents the Holy Spirit. So these images come readily to mind when stimuli from the outside drop from our awareness. The spiritual journey may be represented by such images as a train, bus, plane or boat, any one of which may stand for either a failed or successful voyage. Several of these symbols representing a spiritual journey may appear at once in a dream, especially if the state of prayer continues during sleep.

Another predictable grouping of images includes a door, a gate, a ladder, and a mountain to be ascended. These symbols are most likely to appear when a person is making a choice about whether to go on in prayer. The door usually appears without a handle and one feels no real interest in opening it. Quite often, a brilliant light shines around the edges of the door. Gates and doors are commonly locked and may remain so without a more conscious surrender to Christ than the person has previously offered. More commitment and less self-will are necessary, these images teach us, to unlock the door between God and the soul.

One common feeling at the beginning of this practice is that one is in totally unfamiliar territory, having strange feelings about previously unheard-of experiences. After several tries, however, people usually feel a strong sense of peace, love, and tenderness; at least we found this sense among our retreatants. It may be quite a different matter when one reads about this practice in a book and undertakes the prayer of loving regard alone, without the support of a director or prayer group (and in a spirit of doubt, amusement, or fear). On the other hand, having read about spectacular results enjoyed by others, a reader's expectations may block the process extensively, becoming just another obstacle, another concept that must be surrendered. To avoid such complications, we have rarely told retreatants beforehand what might happen during the prayer of loving regard.

Certain other blockages can interfere with the practice. Sometimes habitually anxious people worry about the prayer of loving regard as they worry about everything else, until they try it a few times. They will usually need a little longer than the others to place themselves in the presence of God before they begin, and should be warned that they may be too tense and preoccupied for immediate results. Once they have relaxed, concentrating on the icon instead of on their anxiety, they will probably be able to practice successfully.

The facial tensions sometimes associated with gazing on the icon, neurologists speculate, are due to the growth of new nerve endings in previously unused sections of the brain, during this unaccustomed process of concentration and sensory deprivation. Classical spirituality calls this phenomenon the development of "spiritual senses." A numbness or tingling frequently appears around the mouth, fingers, and/or shoulders.

As a person enters the night of the senses, he begins to let go of his earliest means of receiving sense data or information. This development is only a passing stage, another step in freedom from the earliest condition of infancy. We are now taking charge of our mental activity and handing over the results to God. Temporary perceptual distortions may give one the feeling of being twelve feet tall or one foot tall. As the physical senses have less and less to do and new "spiritual senses" are growing, some imbalance between the two is likely to occur. Sometimes, too, especially after a very strong experience of being loved, and making a greater commitment to Christ and the Church, a person may feel very unworthy. These feelings of unworthiness, what John of the Cross calls "humbling," are a definite grace. They keep the soul balanced and sane at a time when otherwise it might become intoxicated with pride.

An uncomfortable feeling of emptiness may surface, partly because of the kenotic process of actually emptying thoughts, feelings, attachments, fears, memories, struggles, and worldly goals and values. If a person is not constantly aware of being filled with the Holy Spirit, such an emptiness is painfully felt. The pain is especially noticeable when a person is on a plateau, before he has integrated the earlier experience of God's love. We had retreatants keep detailed journals on the thirty-day retreats, as well as on the one- and two-year retreats. Certain patterns emerged that are described in classical books on spirituality, but often in a language that is not familiar to us today. We observed a cycle of the following stages:

1. Consolation (good sittings with an inflowing of love);
2. Temptation (from Satan or from natural pride);
3. Purification (of old and new imperfections);
4. Integration [often accompanied by life review during prayer time; looks like distraction, but actually is very necessary].

Once the integrative work has been completed, the person moves upward toward a higher plateau, experiencing God's love at first, and then new temptations, appropriate to the new level of awareness, and so the cycle goes on. The process may take place once a month at first, and later once every two months, then perhaps only twice per year, depending on whether growth is slow or fast, on the extent of the person's openness to love, and on the degree of his commitment to the will of God.

During the period of integration, it may seem that nothing is happening in prayer, not only before the icon, but in any other form of prayer. All prayer just seems flat. And only last week, we may think to ourselves, there was such joy in God's presence, such great insights into the Scriptures, such firm resolutions, leaps in purification, and love of neighbor. Now there is nothing, except possibly an increase in irritability, distractions from the past, forgotten memories from childhood, and a suspicion that one has been abandoned by God for some unconfessed sin. Such a state may, of course, indicate a slackening of resolve and love, but often it is a necessary slowing down while the good moments of the past few weeks are being digested. At this time, one needs to stand back and absorb the touch of God into the very bones and atoms of one's whole being. One needs to review one's life drama and faith-history from a new perspective. It is a time of osmosis and growth, but the kind that takes place when one is sleeping or just lying in the sun. The pause usually lasts only a few days.

During retreats of thirty days or longer, we discourage a retreatant from doing any kind of intensive practice at such a slow-down time, and generally reduce new input to a minimum. The apostles who lived with Jesus for three years could have been made into saints in one day—by the same Power that changed water into wine. Yet they were moved by Christ at a pace that corresponded to their own rhythms of faith and doubt, growth and rest.

One should not remain on this integrative plateau for much more than two weeks. If one continues there longer, it is likely that it is not a plateau, but, quite possibly, resistance, fear, and that bit of Jonah that is in every one of us.

Occasionally during icon practice, sexual feelings may arise. Sexual urges during prayer often upset people so much that they stop the prayer for fear of falling into sin. Such surges, with their accompanying images and sensations, are not to be confused with images of spiritual marriage with Christ, such as St. Teresa and St. John describe at the highest stage of contemplative prayer. In spiritual marriage, perfect union is no longer just a happy incident along the way. The fleeting touch of love is replaced by a state of habitual union. One is immersed in God's love like a sponge in the ocean.

If it occurs at all, undirected sexual energy usually occurs in icon practice from twelve to forty-eight hours after a period of progress, prayer, and an intensification of loving commitment to God. At this point, people are often tempted by sexual stirrings. In our work at the Center, we ask them first to renounce these feelings by an act of will, then to perform a prayer practice, the consecration of sexual energies. In this process of moving from rejecting sexuality—individual or collective (or inordinately retaining sexuality), we can eventually experience the divinization of sexuality and hence the divinization of ourselves and the world around us. (See chapter four for a complete study of this practice.) We also call the retreatants' attention to St. Teresa's advice to a relative who had trouble in this area. She reassured him delicately but without false modesty:

> These evil feelings you give me an account of and which happen to you after prayer, should not worry you. I have never experienced anything like that, I admit; the Lord in his goodness has always preserved me from these passions. I imagine that because the soul's joy is excessive, nature must be affected by it. With His Majesty's help this will pass, provided you attach no importance to it. That will not be able to hurt your prayer; the best thing is to pay no attention to it.
>
> *Letters to Lawrence*, 1577

The main point of the prayer of loving regard is not to see any special effects, but to be aware that one is on holy ground, living in light. This light of love fulfills the promise of Jesus in the gospels that He will always be with us. "If anyone love me, he will keep my word, and my Father will love him, and we will come to him and make our abode with him" (John 14:23). This presence, and this alone, is the aim of the prayer of loving regard.

THE PRAYER OF LOVING REGARD

Steps:

1. If a chapel is not available, find a quiet corner, seat yourself comfortably with icon pasted at eye level.

2. Read a scripture passage on light, e.g., John 1:4-5.

3. Do the three steps St. Teresa recommends before beginning any form of prayer: Place yourself in the presence of God; examine your conscience briefly; make the sign of the cross.

4. To ease yourself into a state of mind which is relaxed, not anxious, briefly do the breath prayer (or the heart-to-heart prayer or the consecration of sexual energies). Expect nothing; hope for everything!

5. Gaze into and beyond the icon with no thoughts, no words, no images. . .silently present in this moment with the indwelling Holy Trinity. (A headache may result if the eyes and mind are searching for something. It should be a relaxed, simple gaze, as one might look at a sunset.)

CHAPTER THREE

Freedom, Slavery, and Divinization

> For by these He has granted to us His magnificent promises in order
> that by them you might become partakers of the divine nature...
>
> 2 Peter 1:4

To most of us, the road to contemplation is more likely to cut through
a busy home or office than through a monastery. And most of us cannot
for long enjoy the luxury of quiet, solitary prayer. At least, this is what
we at the Center—Peter and I and our small staff—found during retreats.
Originally we intended to have only a small community of lay contemplatives, but so many unexpected visitors kept coming that we lost our
solitude. In self-defense we instituted two-week retreats, alternating with
a closed-door policy for one month, then enlarged retreats to four weeks.
While we both yearned to be hermits, we raised our three children; verged
on bankruptcy at the end of every month; developed extraordinary skills
in transforming garbage into exotic curries; hitchhiked for miles in snow
and rain; fought with Arctic weather in an uninsulated wooden house;
battled with frozen water pipes; frozen ears, toes, fingers; built exten-
sions on the farmhouse to accommodate our visitors; failed at sheep
farming; succeeded at developing a cottage industry of religious cards;
made friends; made enemies; saw our children molested, kidnapped,
become atheists, become radiant in Christ.

39

Like all our retreatants, we became discouraged, fell and wept lonely tears; were raised up; were sent to Israel by our parents and friends; wrote a book; received retreatants from North America, South America, Ireland, England, Australia, India. Often we were scorned by immediate neighbors, but still we laughed, danced, cried and became despondent; became Carmelite tertieres; lived on social welfare; learned weaving, plumbing, forest management; built hermitages; built a chapel; neglected our dental work; and were blessed beyond words. During these years we began to discover that contemplation was not raptures and ecstasies, not withdrawal from the world, but rather love of God and love of neighbor. After fifteen years, we moved from the farm to Montreal where we remained for three years until we moved to Rome, where we now live, occasionally giving retreats in Santa Barbara and other parts of North America.

The great moments before the icon, like the great moments after having received God in the Eucharist, pass quickly. As we all know, life must go on. How, as the song goes, can we go back to the farm once we have seen Paris? How do we raise children, grow vegetables, keep the books, and put a new roof on the house without leaving the presence of God? The particulars of this hard task will be taken up in chapter five, but here we will work our way through one clear, simple way of seeing ordinary life, in the light of God's love, as we have learned to know it in the moments of contemplation.

The Ignatian "Examination of Consciousness," called here "An Exercise in Awareness," is the form of prayer which we will increasingly be using at the Center to complement the purely contemplative form described in chapter two. (A complete manual of this form of prayer, courtesy of Fr. John English is to be found in the Appendix.) During my own recent experiences with this expanded, modern form of the Ignatian practice, I have learned that our emphasis at the Center on the way God *draws* us to Himself, despite the resistance of our willful nature, is central also to the prayer practice long called "The Examen of Conscience." No longer is this exercise merely a cursory look at whether one has been "good" or "bad" on a certain day, but it is a deep searching into one's awareness of the touch of God in the events of the day and into one's response to them. Contemplation works from the inside out, and the "Examen" works from the outside in. The two work dynamically together, integrating awareness of God's love with Christ-centered action in the world, until one is transformed into the other and no line can be drawn between the two. St. Ignatius's program was originally mystical, not mechanistic, aimed not at making mindlessly obedient Catholics, but at showing both lay and religious contemplatives how to weave their prayer into a seamless cloth with their work lives. It is this simplified modern format of the new examen that will serve as a framework for our discussion of the practical and moral teaching of the Center.

The most obvious way in which we follow the spiritual comings and goings of our many retreatants is the keeping of a journal, which is supposed to document the regular application of their prayer to their lives. As in the revised Ignatian "Exercise in Awareness," the emphasis is not on good works but on an interior responsiveness to the subtle beckonings of God to come closer.

We begin the examen by acknowledging our poverty before God on one hand and our thanksgiving for all He has given us on the other. We call to mind the sorrows of our own slavery "for the evil that I would' not, that I do" (Rom. 7:14-25). We are our own Pharaoh; however, and must not forget that fact. Modern philosophers like Hegel and Marx have been quick to let us off the hook. We are enslaved by church and state, they say; we are enslaved by the family, says Freud. And so on and on. As Berdyaev, the great Russian philosopher, points out, however, the source of slavery is our dependence on the external world for our happiness. [Nikoklai Berdyaev, *Slavery and Freedom*, p. 60] The source of freedom is inside, where Christ told us to look for the Kingdom of God. Give back the interior world to enslaved, modern man, impaled before his television set, stuck in the bogus sensuality of billboards, and he will be free. Whoever wants power over others is a slave; whoever gives it up is free. Whoever sees himself as he is, is free, for the truth has cut his chains. If he projects onto God his own desire to enslave others, he will see God as a slave driver, not a lover, and he will try to placate him by "being good," not by being willing to "be still and know that I am God" (Ps. 46:10), not by being willing simply to love and be silent. The journal is for us, at the Center, one way of loving in silence and acknowledging the need in which our slavery to the external world places us.

At this point it might be a good idea to put this book aside, take up your own notebook and ask yourself some questions about the patterns in your life over which you seem to have no control, but feel uncomfortable. We are all enslaved to something—junk food, alcohol, cigarettes, television, and movies are only a few of the addictions that keep us from confronting ourselves as we are and thanking God for showing us what we really look like in his eyes. In the journals of retreatants we have seen the withering away of many compulsions as soon as they are written down and stared in the face. Enslavements are often only attempts of the ego to keep us from seeing that we aren't God, and that we have no power to run the world. The journal reminds us of our helplessness, of our need, and of God's readiness to give us all we need, in full measure, running over.

My training as a researcher into religious experience at McGill University made me think of asking retreatants to keep detailed journals of exactly what was developing in prayer, in forgiveness, healing, consecration of faculties, significant dreams, and their progress in sanctifying work. Not only did it enable the retreatants and me to see their development, it became a source for training people as spiritual directors. Retreatants kept journals for two-week retreats, four-week retreats, and even for three-year retreats. No one was obliged to leave a journal with us, and everyone had the privilege of refusing to allow it to be read, even anonymously. Without the gracious consent of the many retreatants, we would never have been able to observe the patterns, correlates, and dynamics of many prayer processes to the degree that we did.

The purpose of the journals was to observe developments, detect fears and rationalizations, and help bring obstacles into the light of day, eventually to transform and embrace them in Christ. We would read the journal entries three to four times per day, seven days per week, and write in comments when indicated. We had group direction once a day, and private direction when requested, but usually not more than once every four or five days, depending upon need. For these reasons, we did not develop a system of examination of consciousness, and, in fact, I had never learned a very adequate one, even for myself. I am, therefore, very happy to be able to pass on this extremely valuable prayer practice, developed by the Jesuits at Guelph. (See Appendix VI.)

Journal-keeping for a person who does not have a director may be useful, or it may be quite dangerous. St. Teresa discouraged it, for fear it might make a person self-centered, overly concerned with the vertical way only, with one's exclusive relationship with God. It can also lead to pride and take a person further away from God, becoming another theater for self-deception, an avenue for fantasies. We have found, however, that for modern people the journal is a helpful supplement to being formally directed. When times of desolation set in, and they do, it is encouraging to be able to look back at times of consolation. All of us tend to self-pity and self-dramatization, and an honest journal can go far toward being a corrective for this tendency. Fantasy was minimized at the Center, since we urged that entries be kept brief and were quite specific about their content. Acknowledgment of what specifically has happened in prayer, what errors people see in their lives, and praise to God for what has been given and understood—these are the basic materials of the journals, as they are the first part of the Ignatian exercise.

In the second part of the Exercise in Awareness, the need is to pray for the Holy Spirit's help in seeing clearly how to rise from slavery to freedom. The great stumbling block we have found here is fear, which comes in many guises. One form of fear, of course, is appropriate to the shock we feel on being overwhelmed by the presence of God, the *Mysterium Tremendum*. [Rudolf Otto, *The Idea of the Holy*, chapters 1 and 2] But in the course of the day's work and the night's terrors, we often fall victim to fears that diminish us. Sometimes we bring them masochistically upon ourselves, as when we ride the roller coaster or see a horror film. Other fears we bring on ourselves without meaning to. We are afraid to grow up, afraid to allow our rage or sexual feelings to be exposed and transmuted by the Holy Spirit, afraid to know what is the matter with us, what we are guilty of, why we despair. Some people, according to St. Teresa, even hold back in prayer because they have made up fears to protect themselves from knowing the truth. It is from such fear that we ask the Holy Spirit, during the Examen, to free us. It never ceases to amaze me with what speed the Holy Spirit will honor sincere requests for guidance. The following is from a private journal:

> For several years I had felt bogged down spiritually. I just wasn't moving anywhere. I seemed at a standstill. Even in times of daily Mass, extensive spiritual readings of saints, Scripture study and much personal prayer, there was a nagging suspicion that I was on a treadmill going nowhere. For a while, it seemed that I was in the dark night, but very soon, I realized that was an unsatisfactory "cop-out" explanation. I knew in theory that all of our spiritual

needs are taken care of by simple request, and I continued to pray daily for purity, humility, and submission to God's will, but continued to be bogged down as if my wheels were spinning on slippery ice, moving nowhere, no matter how much gas I applied. One of my favorite musicians, Johnny Cash, was appearing on a Billy Graham Crusade, and I watched the series at first for entertainment but very soon, Billy Graham was prompting me to ponder sin more deeply than I ever had before. It is a fact that I had gone to confession periodically with my laundry list; sincerely repeated the confietor at Mass and even did examination of conscience on a daily basis, but I knew now that I had not broken the back of sin, and sinfulness. I knew that I had been skirting on edges, just enough to feel that I had done the right thing. Now, in earnest, I began to pray every day and all day for the Holy Spirit to instruct me about my sins, especially my secret sins, which I had forgotten or intentionally omitted.

For three weeks I practically locked myself up in my home with this prayer. Saturday night we went to the Russian Orthodox church for vespers to enjoy their beautiful chants, icons, and fragrant incense. Apparently common confession, led by the priest, was observed the first Saturday of every month, after vespers, and we stayed just out of curiosity. The priest knelt down before the congregation, closed his eyes, and prayerfully began his confession! No book. No format. It was enchanting and exhilarating. As he developed the sins of greed, anger, pride, and lust, I started smiling, feeling taller, happier, and more joyful than I had for many, many months. They were all my sins, not his. No longer did I rest in psychologizing away my sins. I was able to accept them as my own responsibility. I felt as if I was starting to float with joy. I felt a cloud of beauty descend upon me and my whole being became filled with light. I was no longer made of skin and bones and flesh, but was filled with a million tiny perfect seed pearls that danced in crystal clear waters and sparkled translucently in sunlight. I felt like a bird soaring above the earth. At last I was free and unchained, a truly liberated woman. What had happened in this process of prayer, petition, grace, and response? For one thing, I stopped holding my parents and my environment resonsible for my sins. I stopped blaming my ignorance, taking responsibility for turning away from Christ since I was four years old. I discarded all the psychological doctrines that excused and justified my sins, and most of all, I admitted that I was a weak, wretched bundle of clay helplessly molded to rebellion and sin. All those distasteful things I had heard for years about sin and the sinfulness of man became suddenly clear, not just old-fashioned, outdated, pre-Vatican dogmas, irrelevant to modern man. They were me. An accurate, realistic description of a disease that was properly diagnosed and could now be treated by the Physician in charge. What joy! What strength! What freedom! What a super surprise! Yet modern psychology had led me to believe that a conviction of sin caused neurotic self-loathing. Instead of feeling like a wretched, repulsive insect, justly despised for my sins by God and man, I felt strong, beautiful, loved, cherished, pure, and moving a step closer to glory! And I began to understand a little more of Paul: "For power is perfected in weakness...I am content with weakness...for when I am weak, then I am strong" [2 Cor. 13]

At the Center our particular way of asking for the light of the spirit to make clear our moment-to-moment actions is the practice of the breath prayer. This prayer doesn't require "time," which people always say they don't have for prayer. It *does* require acknowledgment that we are to "pray unceasingly" (1 Thess. 5:17) and from the heart; we must pray while working, eating, and sleeping; we must write our prayer on our hand, our bedpost, place it at our doorway, like the Jewish Mezuzah.

Prayer in the heart means prayer in one's entire being, so that all one does becomes prayer and no distinctions are made between time for prayer and time for any other activity. A person practicing prayer in this way becomes a walking prayer; his life and being are prayer; praying becomes as vital and necessary as the breath he breathes or the blood that flows through his veins.

In order to experience unceasing prayer in the heart, a person must begin with some form of internalized verbal prayer. An internalized verbal prayer is a prayer that is made up of words, but one that is "spoken" to oneself, over and over again in the mind. The prayer must be in the person's first language, have a representation of God, fit the person's individual spiritual needs at the time, and be so thoroughly satisfying that it will be used without ceasing. The prayer must be short, seven syllables to be exact, because this number most readily coordinates with the rhythm of breathing and other internal rhythms. Seven syllables also make up the length of a person's normal breath. Some examples of this seven-syllable breath prayer are:

I adore You, Son of God.
Not my will, but Thine be done.
Jesus, Healer, make me whole.
I in him and He in me.
Father, Jesus, Spirit—One.
Jesus Christ, I worship you.
In the Name of Jesus Christ.
Jesus, I submit to You.

In choosing an appropriate breath prayer, a beginner should avoid negative words of self-condemnation such as "sinner," "guilt," "sin," etc., unless he fully and completely accepts God's loving forgiveness. Such words and attitudes when repeated over and over using only one's rational introspection can reinforce guilt feelings and easily lead to moroseness and insanity. However, a transcendent reflection, with the Holy Spirit infusing a deep ontological sense of man's creatureliness and sinfulness, leads to freedom and joy. Emphasis on the loving, healing, forgiving, and redeeming aspects of the Christian life will effect positive growth in spirituality. In the words of Saint Bernard of Clairvaux:

Sorrow for sin is indeed necessary, but it should not be an endless preoccupation. You must dwell also on the glad remembrance of God's loving kindness; otherwise, sadness will harden the heart and lead it more deeply into despair.

A person then uses this breath prayer constantly, saying it first out loud, then in silence, continually repeating the phrase in a slow, regular rhythm. With time, the prayer will begin to "say" itself while a person is engaged in any and all activities. As the prayer becomes more and more a part of a person's being, it will enter the unconscious and say itself automatically even during sleep, in accord with the words of the Song of Songs: "I sleep, but my heart waketh" (Song of Songs 5:2) and also the words of Saint Paul: "Pray without ceasing. . . ." (1 Thess. 5:17).

The following examples of how the breath prayer becomes an integral part of a person's daily life are typical responses of individuals who feel the wonderful effects of this ceaseless prayer to God through the power of the Holy Spirit dwelling within them. In the journal of a twenty-four-year-old nurse, whose church attendance record in recent times had been reduced to weddings and bingo games, we see the effects exemplified. Her breath prayer was, "May your presence give me peace."

> My breath prayer stayed with me for most of the time, even while doing dishes and while writing this. I am just using it to close out thoughts and I feel much better—less depressed, less anxious, less alone. Perhaps God has always wanted to be with me, but I have closed him out. [Later] I'm using the prayer instead of a valium, and it worked like a charm. Feel very peaceful and want to laugh. [Later] My feeling of love for people has intensified. [Later] Could feel my heart beating. I was mesmerized by the sound. [Later] My heart pounding, it was like waiting for a dam to break. [Later] During Mass I felt truly joyful and very happy. Can't remember exactly when, but it was a feeling that enveloped my whole being.

In the journal of a fifty-two-year-old priest, who felt unfulfilled in his ministry, we find another example. His breath prayer was "Lord, I come to do Your Will."

> Recited my breath prayer with much ease. Tried rereading the Sermon on the Mount with my breath prayer continuously in mind. [Later] Recited my breath prayer until I fell asleep. Dreams that night were peaceful. None of the usual anger, violence, or hurt feelings. Sometimes I woke up between dreams saying my breath prayer. At other times, as I finished a dream, the breath prayer was said something like a commercial between segments of a TV program. I woke with the alarm, praying my breath prayer. I seem to find a rhythm walking to the bathroom and brushing my teeth. [Later] Had an awesome feeling. I felt I was on the verge of something, I had a sense of burning. [Later] My heart began to radiate and rings of beautiful colors seemed to go out into the room. I took my heart and gave it to N. so that he could use it for his needs. [Later] Saying my breath prayer while shaving and brushing my teeth, I seem lighter and more at peace. [Later] Have learned to practice breath prayer for two minutes between each class and can retain a little of the radiant love for everyone there for a few minutes.

Persons with "no time to pray" can find themselves praying at all times, not with the lips or from a book of prayers, but from the heart, by praying with every breath they take. Such prayer originates in the individual's consciousness, but very soon it becomes so much a part of the person that it is said unconsciously or automatically, during every waking and sleeping moment.

The significance of breath is noted in many places in the Bible, but nowhere more clearly than in Christ's administering of the Holy Spirit to his disciples: "Jesus breathed on them and said, 'Receive the Holy Spirit' " (John 20:22). And St. Bernard emphasizes this indwelling breath of the Spirit as well when he writes:

> Setting His mouth to mine He breathed into it a second time the breath of life, and this time a holier life; for at first He created me a living being; then remade a life-giving spirit.

Without many elaborate details or technical procedures, we saw that the placing of the breath prayer in the heart means centering one's breath prayer in the heart and then centering the heart on God. Spending five to thirty minutes each day alone recollected and consciously saying the breath prayer, while imagining it to be centered in the heart, with the heart centered on God, will help to carry the breath prayer over into all activities of the day. But vigilance is always necessary, keeping a constant remembrance of God within us. St. Bernard reminds us of this need to "watch and pray." "Let Him never find us unprepared when He comes, but always with face uplifted and heart expanded to receive the copious blessing of the Lord...."

People have certainly come to holiness without any marked sensations in their heart or any other part of their bodies. However, we are now referring to the people we have observed doing these particular practices. Some achieve this inner awareness in as little as three hours of practice. For some, longer periods of concentrated practice and opening to the Holy Spirit are necessary. But after an average of fifty hours of such practice, a person usually begins to notice some activity in the heart—a sting or twitch or feeling of expansion in the heart as the efforts of centering prayer in the heart and centering the heart on God begin to bear fruit and prepare him or her for the indwelling grace and action of the Holy Spirit. In time a person will be able to make St. Bernard's hymn of praise his own: "Jesus to me is honey in the mouth, music in the ear, a song in the heart."

HOW TO PRACTICE THE BREATH PRAYER

1. Select an appropriate breath prayer, seven syllables in length, in your first language, with a representation of God that fits your spiritual needs. Emphasize loving, healing, and redeeming.
2. Begin by saying the breath prayer out loud, then over and over to yourself in silence.
3. Center the breath prayer in the heart while centering the heart on God. Imagine that the prayer is going into the heart as you breathe, and direct the desire of your heart toward God.
4. Spend five to thirty minutes each day alone and recollected, consciously saying the breath prayer, imagining it to be centered in the heart with the heart centered on God. Then practice repetition of the breath prayer in the heart during all the activities of your day.

The breath prayer is one practical way we can pay attention to the presence of God in our lives, the whole point of the Ignatian Exercises.

The heart of the Ignatian Examen is to be found in the third section: the seeing of good in all things, even those that keep us from truly trusting God. This means even our fears. There is hardly a spiritual master in the history of Christianity who had as much to say on the subject of fear as Teresa of Avila. In our experience at the Center, we have found that no single emotion is more of an enemy to finding God in the events of daily life, in the experience of prayer, than is this fear; yet of the great masters, only St. Teresa explains why this emotion is such an inhibiting one. Of course fear can be a protection. It can prevent people from taking stupid risks that will endanger their lives. It can also keep people from taking risks that will endanger the ego that they have built up painstakingly over the years, and that they think they would die without.

The Scriptures abundantly use the word *fear*. The Hebrew language has ten words for fear, whereas the English has but one. Reverent fear is quite different from the kind that makes you turn tail and run. Fear of pain is not the same as "caution." Hebrew is truly the language of spirituality; English, commerce; German, philosophy; French, literature; Italian, poetry. that rule has not changed, though so much else has.

Fear is mentioned approximately 400 times in the Bible, about one-third of the remarks being prefaced by "fear not." In Revelation John is told in his vision of Christ, "Fear not, I am the first and the last"

(Rev. 2:17), a quotation frequently used by St. Teresa of Avila. By and large the recommendations in the Old Testament are to fear evil, to fear disobeying God, to fear our own weaknesses, to fear fear itself.

It is hard to imagine how much fear controls us in our spiritual lives. Maslow called it the Jonah complex, but few writers have been clearer on the subject than Rudolf Otto. [See *The Idea of the Holy*, chapter four.] St. John of the Cross came close to rage at spiritual directors who instilled fear into their directees, holding them back from the work of the Spirit. Two examples from our experience at the Center should make this clear.

A few years ago a beautiful young woman with flaming red hair came to visit us. She was an art student and guardedly told us that she wanted to become a nun, a difficult feat since she was not a Catholic and barely knew what it meant to be a Christian. She had been raised in the Canadian north country by a nonbelieving family. Her father, a doctor, was shocked at her proposed vocation and wanted to have her hospitalized in a psychiatric institution—to be cured of her "madness" and become "normal" again. Two professed religious in the immediate famly supported the medical diagnosis and treatment.

Her "symptoms" were that she felt like the Virgin Mary about to give birth to Christ. This sensation was joyful beyond anything she had ever experienced before in her life. Occasionally, while walking in the woods, she would be thrown to the ground and lie there in a thrilling rapture for an hour. The whole world was bathed in a golden light and even ugly things became radiantly beautiful. At such times she loved everyone without reserve, including some people she had formerly despised. She could not kill insects or eat meat, and yearned to die even when she was most happy. "Worst" of all, she wanted to leave art college, go into the seclusion of a convent, and think of nothing ever again except God. Her parents succeeded in having her hospitalized and drugged senseless for many months. She, in turn, succeeded in deceiving her doctors and nurses into thinking that she was really taking the medications instead of flushing them down the toilet. She became skilled in basket weaving, was able to convince her captors that her visiting spiritual director was a second cousin, covered her Bible to make it look like a murder mystery, kept her feelings secret, and thus achieved her release within a year. The hospital records show that her "incurable schizophrenia" was cured by a new "miracle drug."

Another woman who came to visit us at about the same time was a professor of philosphy, a married woman with two children. As soon as she could get us alone, she wept pitifully for half an hour and told us her tale of horror. A devout Catholic convert for several years, she had for some time experienced a new depth of joy in prayer, but had visions accompanied by boats, angels, oceans, crosses, and various imagery completely incomprehensible and frightening to her. She mentioned them all in confession and was advised to seek psychiatric help. Her confusion, shame, and fear resulted in her losing twenty-five pounds in a few weeks, and she lived in constant agony. When she finally found a director of some skill, she was able to regain a sense of balance, but she just missed being shattered beyond human help.

Such misunderstanding of the dynamics of spirituality is not exclusive to psychiatrists, nor to the parish priests. Nor is it a present-day phenomenon. St. John of the Cross devotes many pages to this subject, and accuses incompetent spiritual directors of being more of an obstacle than the devil.

What is the answer to fear? It is love, as St. Ignatius understood in his Examen; it is "finding the good in all things." We are not, the psychiatrist and spiritual director Gerald May assures us, to expect unconditional love from others. [Gerald May, *Will and Spirit*, Harper and Row, New York, 1982, pp. 137-9] Neither a parent's love nor a spouse's will be available to us all the time. Because we know this fact, with much pain, we assume that God, too, loves us with merely conditional love, and that if we aren't good enough to earn that love, we won't have it. If we suffer loss, we assume that we have earned God's anger; if we ask for favors, we assume God will want to reward us for good behavior, as though our life were a prison and He the warden. We need to rework our own understanding of what God is for us. He is a mother as well as a father. As Julian of Norwich wrote:

> As verily as God is our Father, so verily God is our Mother, and
> that shewed He in all, and especially in thee sweet words where
> He saith: I it am. That is to say, I it am, the Might and the Good-
> ness of the Fatherhood; I it am, the Wisdom of the Motherhood;
> I it am, the Light and the Grace that is all blessed Love; I it am,
> the Trinity; I it am, the Unity; I it am; I am the sovereign Good-
> ness of all manner of things, I am that maketh thee to love; I am

that maketh thee to long; I it am, the endless fulfilling of all true
desires.

To love God is to love not with the brains, but with the heart's passionate commitment, a commitment of one's entire humanity, which over-
rides fear. As in the Ignatian exercise, one must ask the question, "Did
I see Christ in the other today?" "Did I see Him in the events around
me?" These are the questions we ask in our practice of the heart-to-
heart prayer, one which answers the questions of the Ignatian Exercise:
"How am I being drawn to Christ in love?"

With some embarrassment and worry, we offered contemplation of
the Sacred Heart to people at the Center, knowing that they might regard
this picture of Christ's heart being hung above their icon as a mere valen-
tine. Far from being a pious going-through-the-motions, this practice
can be shatteringly powerful. It is based on the authoritative power of
Christ and often is an explosive experience for those who submit to the
transforming power of Jesus within them. Far from being a sentimental
reverie, heart-to-heart prayer has as its goal to open the hearts of prayerful
people to the consuming fire of God's love, made known to all through
the perfect love exemplified in the heart of Christ.

From the two-week journal of a skeptical thirty-five-year-old priest, who taught high school physics, and who was asked to contemplate
a picture of Christ's Sacred Heart, instead of his icon:

> Felt a strange pressure at heart. [Later] Many currents to heart.
> [Later] Strange currents in chest, several rising currents and than
> a current that started small in chest, then grew larger and larger.
> [Later] Many currents to heart, deep sense of compassion, yet not
> mine. I think it is the Lord's compassion if that is possible. [Later]
> Currents of much longer duration, spreading out in all directions.
> Felt a joy that was deep but not the bubbly kind of joy. On the verge
> of tears.

After the prayer of the lips and the mind has been centered in the
heart, and after some practice in offering sexual energy to God (see chapter four), a person is then ready to begin heart-to-heart prayer. The technique of this practice should not be begun until there is some manifestation
of heart activity or awareness of the heart from the previous two prac-

tices, no matter how slight that activity may be. This is chiefly to prevent early discouragement, although there are cases of persons responding to this last practice when they did not respond to the previous practices.

In order to make clear the approach to be taken in practicing heart-to-heart prayer, two analogies are appropriate. Most persons are familiar with the term "having a heart-to-heart talk." What does this phrase imply? Two persons speaking in a warm, intimate, personal, and honest way, each with complete selfless regard and genuine conern for the other characterizes the nature of such a human encounter. A heart-to-heart talk demands the fullness of affective response in both persons, and implies immediate and forthright honesty in expressing feelings and emotions.

In a similar way, heart-to-heart prayer involves a giving of all our heart in complete honesty and selflessness to the Radiant Heart of Christ, a heart that has loved us to the point of death, in order that we may have life. In the Gospel of St. John, Christ prays that our life may be complete in Him. "Make your home in me, as I make mine in you" (John 15:4). This living in Christ is nothing other than a complete reorientation of love and a total transformation of the heart in Christ's heart. Again our Lord prayed, "May they all be one, Father. . .as you are in me and I am in you. . . ." (John 17:21). The life and loving relationship of the Father with the Son is thus made available for every Christian who is faithful enough to invite Christ into his heart and to dwell himself in the Sacred Heart of his Lord.

The method is simple. Seat yourself in front of a picture of Christ and his Radiant Heart. Then visualize an inflowing from Christ's heart into your own heart and a resultant exchange of energy and love between hearts. Although a person may not at first experience what feels like love, by concentrating on a simple prayer such as "I in Him and He in me," throughout the sitting, one will eventually come to an experience of divine love in an intimate and personal way. With practice a person will come to experience this liberation in divine love in all aspects of daily life and not exclusively during formal sittings in front of a picture of Christ's Radiant Heart.

The following examples are the experiences not of accomplished proficients, but of people who began with a prayerful wilingness to meet God heart to heart by this prayer practice. In the four-week journal of a forty-five-year-old nun who had been experiencing a crisis of faith not long before beginning heart-to-heart prayer, we find:

> I used the image of the Sacred Heart and experienced a constant
> beat in my heart. I just drank it in. I was receiving everything. Later
> I held the people dearest to me in my heart. I have a sense of ache
> now. It is like being aware of having exercised something new for
> quite awhile. [Later] Had the desire to continue this new medita-
> tion throughout the day. Became conscious of Christ's ever-flowing
> source of love.

From the four-week journal of a forty-two-year-old priest:

> Experienced a great expansion in my chest again as I desired to
> be filled with all the creative life energies so that my heart would
> open wide, let the energies flow over into the Heart of God and
> return to me. I had the feeling of being filled and exploding in the
> center part of my body. How did each of these people come to such
> a close, personal identification with Christ?

Very recently my husband, Peter, brought to my attention the description of profouund prayer experience with a picture of Christ in Teilhard
de Chardin's book *Hymn of the Universe*. [Teilhard de Chardin, *Hymn
of the Universe*, Harper and Row, New York, 1965. See Appendix V.]
This description sounded so much like the experiences that retreatants
had at the Center that I had to laugh out loud. It was complete with
rainbow colors, neon-like radiance, and eyes filled with boundless love.
Chardin does not mention the usual first response to this experience:
"It must be an optical illusion; the lighting in the room changed while
I was doing the practice; I must be imagining it."

Many Christians feel drawn to and identify with an image of the
historical Christ. They "see" Christ in history, preaching and healing
the sick; they feel drawn to this historic person, seeking to imitate his
compassionate ways, his great love for men. If they are drawn with sufficient admiration, these Christians then further seek to become disciples, to follow Christ more closely and to live by his words, making
the Gospel not only a message, but a way of life. Still Christ remains
distant to them, a person removed from our reality by two thousand years.
Although his teaching may live in these persons, this Christ of history
is, in a sense, a dead Christ, for out of love for humanity, Christ offered

his own humanity in atonement for sins.

The reality of the Risen Lord, who transcends time and history, offers more than a model to be imitated, more than discipleship, more than remembrances from the past. The glorified Christ of the Resurrection melts away the distance of history and calls us to union with the Father through the love of Christ and by the power of the Holy Spirit. As Christ is the Vine, we are the branches intimately and vitally linked to Him, drawing life and nourishment from the living waters which flow in abundance from his breast.

If we prepare his way in ourselves, Christ will come to us, make his home in us, and exchange his heart for our heart, his mind for our mind, and his strength for our strength. His union with us is a marriage indeed, and two can truly become one flesh.

In the second book of Kings, Yahweh admonished his people for pursuing the emptiness of idolatry and infidelity to his covenant. "They pursued emptiness, and themselves became empty through copying the nations round them although Yahweh had ordered them not to act as they did" (2 Kings 17:15). The situation is much the same today, as the new people of God pursue the emptiness of nations and idolatry in its many contemporary forms. But those who seek God with a pure heart can find Him, not outside themselves but in the sanctuary within, on the altar of the heart. And finding Christ dwelling within, they will simultaneously discover Christ's love dwelling not only within themselves, but in all men; his light shines on all men, radiating love in all, through all, and with all, to the glory of God the Father. The heart-to-heart prayer is a means to this end.

THE HEART-TO-HEART PRAYER

Steps:
1. Begin with scripture reading, preferably from the Gospel of St. John, with reference to God's indwelling of man.,
2. Center breath prayer in the heart for a few minutes.
3. Raise sexual energy into the heart for a few minutes (see chapter four).
4. Seated in front of a picture of Christ and his Radiant Heart, visualize an inflowing from Christ's heart into your own heart and a resultant exchange of energy and love between hearts.

Having seen Christ dwelling within, in a heart-to-heart relationship, we cannot help entering the next phase of the Christian prayer experience—contrition and sorrow. We see ourselves as we are and in the divine perspective, as Christ sees us. At this point in our retreatants' development, we ask them to undergo a ritual familiar to Charismatics—the healing of memories.

Nothing will ever quite equal the thrill, joy, and excitement Peter and I experienced on the thirty-day retreats, watching and intimately sharing how God was working and forming people's lives. As I look back, the retreatants appear to me like dancers in a vast ballet. They unfold like flowers, coming forth, pulling back, falling down, reaching the stars, blooming into glory. The conductor, of course, without whom things collapse very rapidly, is the *choregos*, the leader of the dance, a name formerly used for the Holy Spirit. An integral part of this dance of life was the process called "the healing of memories." We used Agnes Sanford's book *The Healing Light* (Logos International, Plainfield, N.J.) as required reading prior to a retreat, and used her tapes on the introductory lecture. Because Catholics are used to the Sacrament of Reconciliation, in which they confess *their* sins, it was a little disconcerting for some of them to be told that in the healing of memories they were only to forgive those who had sinned against them. The process is not intended as a replacement for the Sacrament of Penance (Reconciliation) but as a supplement to it.

We recommended that a person examine several years of his or her life and submit the most traumatic events for healing in the evening, at the time of Exposition of the Blessed Sacrament. It was always a remarkable, new, and fresh experience for us to see how God would rapidly heal wounds and bind broken hearts. My own major healing process took three years to complete. By completion, I mean that I not only had to be taught how to forgive, but how to see Christ in my "enemy," a raper of children.

In the early years at the Center, before this practice was so widespread, it was common for people to deny that they had any need for healing. Even if they were receptive to the process, I had to warn them not to expect that total healing could always take place in a half an hour. They would need to repeat and relive the healing daily in their preparation for prayer, sometimes for months, before the breakthrough into forgiveness and health took place.

Every practice has its hazards and the danger of this one is that people can remain indefinitely on the level of "magic." Once the magic show of healing is over, they get bored with God. Others, unfortified by adequate theology and scriptual study, can get caught up in being instruments for the healing process. They see all illness and suffering as a result of unconfessed sins. This kind of judgment has left many people more discouraged, sick, and depressed than before they encountered the healing ministry.

We explain these points briefly to people before they take part in the healing of memories session, through which they are led by a staff member who is trained to bring up precisely those sufferings that we can be sure will find specific echoes in the souls of the individuals. Who has not, at times, felt unloved by a parent? Rejected by a friend? Unfairly treated at school or work? We are much less singular in our griefs than we think we are, and the healing of memories practice takes account of this commonality of suffering.

Those who sit in the chapel before the Blessed Sacrament waiting to begin the healing, are reminded that it is important to spend the allotted time dealing with wounds they have suffered, not wounds they have dealt others. "Ask to be shown," we tell them, "all the wounds of the past, not discriminating between major and minor ones. Don't pass over a hurt just because 'It wasn't her fault' or 'He was just doing what he thought best.' " If you are stabbed and bleeding, you will need stitches just as urgently, whether a friend accidentally stabbed you or you were maliciously struck down by the knife of a mugger. The wound is equally damaging in both cases. Above all, don't try to accomplish any of this by your own power. Rely on Christ, on his infinite power and love, for healing and wholeness. We also ask the retreatants to divide the number of years of their lives by the number of days in the retreat. The number arrived at will be the number of years covered each evening, at the time of the Adoration of the Blessed Sacrament, working backward from the present.

Of all the people we most need to forgive, it turns out not to be the one who hated us the most, but the one who probably loved us the most, our mother. How often it turns out that she panicked upon learning of her pregnancy, or even felt fear mixed with desire for a wanted child. During the nine months of gestation, we picked up her anxiety, her fatigue, her angers and fears, and then we experienced the ultimate insult and violence—expulsion and rejection from the womb. Even the most loving mother nursing her child at the breast is unable to still every cry, satisfy every want, and fill every demand. It is usually the loving mother who takes her child to the doctor to be pierced by needles and to the dentist to be x-rayed and have cavities filled. It is the mother who expells the child from the sanctuary of the home to go to school on wintry days. All these events, good in themselves, are experienced by the child as violations and betrayal, thus breeding resentment and distrust. The same mother protected us from injuries and spanked us for running out into traffic. All of these benevolent actions, as well as the more obvious human failings, need to be forgiven in the healing of memories process.

On a deeper level, we all seem to accuse our mother for having infected us with "sinfulness" or whatever we perceive within ourselves that prevents us from having that closeness to God that would be divine bliss. Only after a total and complete forgiveness of our mother can most of us then return to the Mother of us all, Mary, and absorb her divine motherhood in the way we need it most for our sanctification. The same depth and detail of forgiveness applies also to our fathers, to free us to experience the complete circle of love from God to us, then from us to God, and from God through us to others.

The process of healing of memories takes about one-half hour and can be done during Adoration each day.

THE HEALING OF MEMORIES

Steps:

1. Remind yourself of the loving presence of Christ in the Blessed Sacrament.

2. Ask the Lord to open your mind and heart to see the hidden as well as the more visible wounds that need healing.

3. Look back over the time period in question. With each incident that comes to mind, go through these three steps:

> a. Ask Christ to heal you of that wound and any scars you may be carrying from it.
>
> b. Ask Him to heal the one who wounded you.

c. Ask Him to forgive the other, out of his infinite forgiveness, through you.

4. Take as little or as much time as you need.
5. At the end of the session, ask Christ for healing of anything in that time period that lies forgotten but may still be wounding you.
6. Later, when you make your journal entry, just note the years you co-vered that night and if you experienced any difficulty. Otherwise, note briefly any comment you may have.

We were interested mainly in seeing to what extent the retreatants were able to see the healing presence of Christ travelling with them through their lives, not just in autobiographical details. As we read journal after journal, we saw similar patterns of pain relived with tears, fol-lowed by a joyful sense that God was wiping the tears away.

One forty-year-old priest will serve as an example for hundreds. Pierre M. was a seminary teacher who wanted to be healed of his "in-ner involvements" and to "rest in the Lord." (A complete text of Fr. Pierre's journal entries on the healing of memories, with Peter's com-ments, can be found in Appendix IV.) For a few years he had been a Discalced Carmelite, and still longed for the silence of the contempla-tive life. He was surprised to learn during the healing of memories that he was still enslaved by resentment and bitterness against people who had hurt him. He writes: "I placed them in the fire of Jesus's heart-furnace to burn them, then offered my wounded self to Jesus in the Eu-charist to be healed." Later in the month he went deeper into his past pain. "Tears, or, rather, sobbing poured out of me. All the rejections and hurts I have experienced in all my life came before me and I wept in my desolation. Pent-up tears. Freeing tears. Healing tears. Then the Word of God within me very clearly: "I know you. I love you. I am with you as I have been every step of your life." Tears of gratitude, un-belief, yet total conviction of this tremendous love. Toward the end of the month he writes, with obvious relief, "When I went outside at eleven, the world was new. Everything was a revelation of God. Immense joy. I laughed aloud."

The joy felt by Father Pierre upon experiencing the healing of memories is characteristic of people we have seen who have moved from slavery to freedom. Ordinarily they are also going to Confession regu-larly during the retreat and are experiencing the Sacrament of Recon-

ciliation, along with the healing, sorrow over sin, and loving forgiveness for those who have sinned against them. They are particularly ready
to work on the fifth and last phase of the Examen of Consciousness,
which is a hopeful resolve about the future action and attitude, involving a positive acceptance of one's freedom, reconciliation, and the joyful process of becoming more like the image of God they were created
to be.

After the healing, they find themselves ready to "leave the past behind, and with hands outstretched to whatever lies ahead . . . go straight
for the goal" (Phil. 3:13). Like St. Paul's runner and St. Teresa's warri-
or, they struggle not in hate or anger, but in love. Having experienced
the love of God directly in prayer, it becomes for them a touchstone
of unconditional love in their daily lives.

One of the most common questions people have after an intense
experience of God's love is: How can it be that only one weekend has
passed since I felt God's love so strongly I could die immediately for
Him, and yet I am showing no greater love for people than before, probably less? The answer lies partly in the Scriptures—in the life of St.
Peter, for example. He had intense love for Christ, but also an intense
need for approval and acceptance from people. Some kinds of plants
bear fruit very soon after blooming, like beans; other plants, like apple
trees, take seven years to bloom. Also, very often after an intense love
experience, we want privacy with the beloved and resent any invasion
of this privacy, especially from people who are expecting some kind
of concentrated attention. At a time like that it is much easier to show
affection to kittens than to people. (We had some of the most loved kittens in the province, I am certain.)

Another kind of question that is frequently asked is: How is it that
I seem to be falling in love with trees and plants and animals? Here Isaiah
gives us a clue about the unitive feeling with plants and animals as the
boundaries of the ego begin to enlarge and take in more of God's creation (Is. 2:6-9).

Most people, regardless of how much their mind knows about God,
are surprised by that kind of direct, positive, existential, personal proof
of God's love when it comes into their own being. They are usually surprised when their love is expanded to other objects and people, and need
time to learn how to use this new love with discretion and without en-
dangering themselves or others. The love experience can be accompa-

nied by intense purification and forgiveness of all injury so that a person is as vulnerable as a new-born chicken.

Take this example from the journal of a 35-year-old mother and housewife:

> As I looked behind me in the theatre from my second row, I was amazed at the intense waves of love that were flowing from the people in the rows behind me. As my eyes climbed backward to the rows further and further away, the love kept on pouring into me, until I could not bear it without clutching my breast. Even from the balconies upstairs, the love was surging without control. I had been quite. . .contemptuous of these people, these stupid masses who behave like animals in a pen. I had always been contemptuous of people who sat in seats further back and cheaper than mine. Now, they were all so beautiful, like sweet children, with innocence, warmth, purity, and holiness. I was terrified and fought off all that love as much as I could. I was comfortable hating, competing, fighting. The very last thing I wanted was to love anyone, let alone love everyone without any distinction. [Later] There is something very strange in the way I feel about people. I can't get angry with anyone, not even a child-molester who has been abusing local girls, including my daughter. All I can do is pity him for having to stoop to such behavior; it seems so stupid and risky. I can't bring myself to join the other mothers who want to have him beaten up and have his legs broken. I can't even agree to report him to the police. I just feel sorry for him. [Later] When I was living that summer in the farmhouse, alone with the three children, my neighbors had strongly recommended that I have a shotgun in full view to discourage unwelcome men and thieves or drunkards out for fun. I knew I couldn't use a gun on anyone, and though my doors did not yet have locks, I couldn't figure out how to protect my children in case of danger. I tried holding a pair of scissors in my hands to see if I could carry them in my pocket and use them for self-defense, but there was absolutely no way I could have used them. I would have preferred death. One night I discovered a man in my bed in the bedroom I shared with my youngest daughter. He was passed out drunk, or pretending—I never knew [which]. I just somehow got him out. It took three hours.

Such a story, very common in one variation or another for those who feel divine love intensely, indicates how difficult it is to balance prudence with love, how hard it is to love the person and hate the situation.

For years I kept seeing everyone as a saint or a potential saint. It was a long time before I was comfortable with my own judgment. Most people don't experience these extremes, nor do they have to make these kinds of decisions. But many moved from a world where survival of the fittest was the bottom line, to the Center, where they were rapidly thrust into an ocean of divine love, and sometimes almost drowned in it. Protection is clearly needed for those who are walking out from the chapel into the real world.

The safest route to take when one has intense experiences is repeated use of the sacraments, a spiritual director when possible, a prayer group for support, and a spiritual companion with whom to share.

The most serious danger after an intense religious experience, whether a unitive one of love, a greater heartfelt commitment to Christ, deepening of understanding of the Scriptures, or even physical healing, is the the pull backward by Satanic forces. It is rarely obvious to the person involved, and certainly not to be taken lightly. It remains to be seen which is Satan's greatest victory—convincing people that God does not exist or that Satan does not exist. Many people accept so much of what Christ and the apostles taught us, try to live by it at great sacrifice and with personal pain, yet refuse to accept what Christ said about Satan and his encounters with Satan.

"Put on the armor which God provides," St. Paul writes in Ephesians 6:11-18, "so that you may be able to stand firm against the devices of the devil . . . for our fight is not against human foes, but against cosmic powers, against the authorities and potentates of this dark world." St. Paul urges the Ephesians to wear truth, integrity, faith, and salvation as protections against diabolic onslaughts. Some modern Christians might prefer not to hear that a powerful, disembodied entity is far more their enemy than the person or situation that seems to be threatening them at work. Nevertheless, the Scriptures and our experience in dealing with people at the Center make it very clear that dropping our defenses before God in contemplative prayer also makes us vulnerable to Satanic influence. For this reason, we encourage the building of strong habits of virtue (St. Paul's armor) in conjunction with contemplative prayer.

Neurologists tell us that a habit is broken in about twenty-one days. To make sure we had given retreatants long enough to "dehabituate" from destructive patterns, we gave them an extra week. Thirty days of total immersion is the length of time that psychologists have found it necessary to learn a new language at the unconscious level. After thirty days, a student can read, think, and dream in the new language. Likewise, within thirty intensive days, all the prayer practices will have been wound into one cord, each strand being originally one kind of prayer.

The breath prayer will have gone into the heart and even throughout the body; the heart-to-heart prayer will have been combined with the consecration of sexual energies (see chapter four); the icon will have been used outside of the chapel, perhaps in the kitchen or while doing laundry; and most people will have found a glimpse, at least, of God in others and in themselves.

And so they come to the end of the retreat, as to the end of the Ignatian Examen, with a firm resolve to watch for the action of God in their lives, and to be as continually aware of Him while working as they are while praying, to weave the life of the body totally together with the life of the spirit, so as to make one seamless garment.

CHAPTER FOUR

The Consecration of the Body to God

Lead me back again to thy likeness Refashioning my ancient beauty.
from the Orthodox service

If a person from a foreign culture who had never seen a football game observed an athlete's behavior, he would indeed think him a masochist. If this foreign visitor were to see the athlete knocked down violently during a football game, he would be sure the athlete was insane to bring this pain upon himself. The athlete seems to the observer merely to be suffering. The only safe place seems to be on the benches in the grandstand, watching. But look again. Watch the ecstatic hugs the players give each other when the goal is made, the game is won. They would tell you that such joy is bought only by suffering and that such suffering, for the end of winning, is only joy.

So it goes with prayer. We are surrounded by people from "foreign cultures" who try to discourage us by their ignorance, ridicule, personal fears, blindness, inertia, scorn, and their quite understandable desire to pamper the body rather than train it. Should they be surpised when, like a spoiled child, the body turns on them?

As in a football game, the players on the prayer field are few and the grandstand is teeming with hordes who cheer, drink beer, and consume bags of potato chips. The victory they like to think is theirs is only an illusion, like the passing pleasure of watching the ball fly between the goalposts. The real fight is inside themselves, and that's what genuine asceticism is all about.

Asceticism can take positive or negative forms. In negative asceticism, a person makes up a list of resolutions, vices, and obstacles that he determines to renounce, after which he expects to find God and bliss. In positive asceticism, one pursues God; and the vices, inordinate attachments, and obstacles drop away. Our experience at the Center has been that in a large percentage of people, positive asceticism is the most effective way to change. People become radically transformed after the experience of being with God, and their enslavements to negative attitudes, resentments, fears, and hates drop away. Sometimes the dropping away is only temporary, but quite often, it is permanent.

Over the years we have found at the Center that a middle path is the safest. Some negative asceticism, at least as far as ordinary morals go, is necessary. Some things simply must be given up, painful as the giving up may be, in order to let the body mature and share in the promised resurrection. We all know, if we are honest as we look at our lives, what those things are.

No book, no liturgy, no theologian, not even the Scriptures, can illustrate the experience of *kenosis* (the emptying of ourselves in order to be filled by God), more graphically than people who describe, in books and TV interviews, how they "died." In their "death" they see a brilliant light that beckons them into the greatest joy and bliss and then are reluctantly brought back to life by a medical team. I have seen these people angry, grieving, or simply lost and depressed after such an experience. In many cases, previously ignorant of religious teachings, they now believe that no harm will come to them in death. Often they long to die and return to the bliss they have momentarily touched. Ordinary life seems to be just marking time. This longing to abandon the body is asceticism in its most extreme form. It is by no means masochistic or suicidal, even though it may look as though all normal prudence has been forgotten in the desire for God, as seemed to be the case with St. Therese of Lisieux. Such extremes are not necessary for most of us. What is required is that we die to the self in order to be reborn, so that the stone will be rolled away from the tomb, allowing the resurrection of the body that Christ promised would happen. Whether or not we like it, incarnational Christianity means honoring the body as the vessel of

God.

The next pages are written for those who are not content to treat the spiritual life as a spectator sport like hockey or football. They want to get into the arena and do the playing. They are excited at the challenge, at the goals, the victory. No price is too high for them to pay. They are prepared to undergo rigorous training: fasting, relentless coaching, little sleep, much practice. If you have ever watched a football player sweat out 100 push-ups, run five miles, do half an hour of weight lifting, and one hour of ballet dancing, you might think he was suffering. But is he? Is he denying himself? Punishing himself? He would not say so. He would say he is getting stronger, healthier, lighter, more agile, more competent, and closer to his goal, clsoer to victory. Like St. Paul, he would say he is building strength so that he can win the race.

Only by throwing our whole being into the ocean of God can we learn how to swim in this fearful element. Only then can we know that which holds us up, keeps us from drowning, is the salt of our tears, and the water of life. In this ocean we pull off our shoes, our clothes, all that we thought necessary for survival. We breathe the air of grace, which is all we need for life.

For some time psychologists have been telling us that we project the sin in our own minds onto other people. Hitler persuaded Germans to blame the Jews for their economic troubles; many Americans blame the Blacks for their crime rate. All of us are guilty of putting the blame conveniently somewhere else so we won't have to change, repent, or make reparation for our faults. If the deep soul-searching done in faithful practice of the Examen is really to be of use, however, it must serve as a pitilessly faithful mirror of our real face. We must see that we put the blame everywhere but where it belongs, squarely on our own minds. We have especially blamed our bodies, the temples of the Holy Spirit (as the Scriptures call them), for our selfish egotism, our desire to serve our own will rather than God's, which is our way of avoiding the sacrifices demanded by love.

The body can't talk back, except by getting sick, so the mind can "safely" treat it like a slave. It has done so throughout the history of Christian asceticism. Though Jesus stressed the incarnational union of God and his creation, we ourselves have continually chosen to punish the body for the sins of the mind. The recent work of theologians like Margaret Miles reminds us that early Christians were by no means as

frightened of the body as seventeenth-century Jansenists (our direct fore-
bears) were, and that the body must be made not only a partner in prayer, but fully divinized, lest it become a silent enemy, sabotaging the effort of the spirit to know itself fully.

Genuine asceticism exists now as always to bring the body and the
mind into harmony so that both can participate in the vision of God.
Since participation must include the embodiment of that vision here on
earth ("Let your light so shine before men that they may glorify your
Father who is in Heaven" [Matt.5:16]), we as Christians have the gift,
the grace, and the duty to join our body to the work of the soul.

No one is clearer than John of the Cross [*The Spiritual Canticle*,
p. 547] in describing the goal of true asceticism, that joyful discovery
of oneself in God's beauty:

> And let us go forth to behold ourselves in Your beauty. This me-
> ans: Let us so act that by means of this loving activity we may at-
> tain to the vision of ourselves in Your beauty in eternal life. That
> is: That I be so transformed in Your beauty that we may be alike
> in beauty and both behold ourselves in Your beauty, possessing now
> Your very beauty; this, in such a way that each looking at the other
> may see in the other his own beauty, since both are Your beauty
> alone, I being absorbed in Your beauty; hence, I shall see You in
> Your beauty, and You shall see me in Your beauty, and I shall see
> myself in You in Your beauty, and You will see Yourself in me in
> Your beauty; that I may resemble You in Your beauty, and You
> resemble me in Your beauty, and my beauty be Your beauty and
> Your beauty my beauty; wherefore I shall be You in Your beauty,
> and You will be me in Your beauty; and therefore we shall behold
> each other in Your beauty.
>
> This is the adoption of the sons of God, who will indeed declare
> to God what the very Son said to the Eternal Father through St.
> John: "All my things are yours, and yours mine" (John 17:10). He
> says this by essence, since He is the natural Son of God, and we
> say it by participation, since we are adopted sons. He declared this
> not only for Himself, the Head, but for His whole mystical body,
> the Church, which on the day of her triumph, when she sees God
> face to face, will participate in the very beauty of the Bridegroom.
> Hence the soul makes the petition that she and her Bridegroom
> go forth to behold each other in His beauty.

It is true, of course, that we are going to have to give up our bodies someday, at least our bodies as we have known them. At times mystics, like dying people, think they have left the body and their individual selves behind them forever. Being in our bodies reminds us that we are not God, nor even "one with Him," strictly speaking, yet divinization of the body begins on Earth. Naturally we would rather not acknowledge such a "limitation." Yet, there it is, the experience all of us have, just as we all wake from dreams.

Once we have stopped blaming the body for our problems, we become as tender toward it as mothers. Is our attitude one of Manichean or Jansenist contempt? Is our body complaining to us about our indifference? Is it crying for rest? We must look carefully at our compulsions and our unreasonable demands and then take time to sleep, eat wholesome food, hug our children, weed our gardens. We need to take brisk walks, move our muscles with gentle, persistent regularity, pray as we walk, dance, and work. Of all the parts of us apparently most resistant to resurrection, the sexual aspect is perhaps the most obvious. We live in a culture where sex is the avenue of thrills, ego-affirmation, pride, and worship. If we can do nothing else, at least we can have sex and feel important, even transported into a moment where we briefly forget ourselves and feel like gods.

Sexuality is an experience that the Christian, whether married or celibate, must deal with squarely , not allowing pseudo-worship, Manichean contempt, or self-importance to get in his or her way. Because Jesus held up marriage as a metaphor of God's relationship with the soul, we, too, must look seriously at that sacramental institution as the model for our love of God.

The role of sexuality in the Christian life has undergone many changes in recent years. Although it is the only major religion in the world that views marriage as a sacrament and forbids arranged marriages, Christianity is only beginning to rediscover the deeper understanding of man's sexual nature. Many prejudices and preconceptions still exist, and a genuine understanding of the creative energies within man and creation needs to be developed, experienced, and integrated into a Christian understanding of self. If Christians realize the sanctifying power of sexuality and are able to recognize the sacredness of sex in their lives, then a prayerful theology of sexuality can develop that will enrich the deepest aspects of man's creative existence. A technique of prayer practice at the Center called "consecration of sexual and creative energy into the heart" (formerly known as "lifting of sexual energy into the heart") makes possible the realization that sexual energy is creative energy to be used in the service of God and our own divinization.

Within Christianity a negative interpretation of chastity has hindered normal spiritual development and has resulted in the fear of sexual energies by both married persons and celibates. A culture that degrades celibacy also tends to degrade sacramental marriage and vice versa. Historically, they are complementary states, mutually dependent on each other. If marriage were only a necessary evil, an accommodation of ugly, animal urges, then celibacy would scarcely be a virtue. It is no virtue, after all, to flee a misfortune. No, the pattern of selfless love on which Christ modeled his love for the Church is as much a gift of God as is virginity.

For all Christian persons, married as well as celibate, the need exists for a prayerful theology of sexuality. Such a theology needs to be defined by practice and experience, as well as by theory and dogma.

Philip Sherrard in *Christianity and Eros* quotes St. John Climacus on the transmutation of sexual love:

> A certain man, seeing a woman of unusual beauty, glorified the Creator for her; the mere sight of her moved him to the love of God and made him shed a flood of tears. It was indeed astonishing to see how what for another could have been a pitfall to perdition was for him the supernatural cause of a crown of glory. If such a man, on similar occasions, feels and acts in the same way, he is risen, and is incorruptible, even before the general resurrection.

Sherrard points out that a proper understanding of the nature of sexuality is not to be confused with contemporary forms of sexual expression and exploitation. Western culture is saturated with the strictly carnal aspects of sexuality, but sexual energy per se penetrates all of creation and is the creative, energizing, life-giving force that permeates and vitalizes all of nature. Sexual love is the model for divine love and, at times, vice versa.

The Song of Songs expresses the ancient Hebrew conviction that sexual expression is a school for knowing God. For the Jews, the action of *Ruah*, spirit-in-motion, united with the flesh of man in a perpetual incarnation. Unlike the Greeks, the Jews did not see spirit and flesh as enemies. The Zohar, a primary source of Jewish mysticism (of which St. Teresa was almost certainly aware), taught that bad habits should be broken, not repressed. Only those habits that hurt spiritual growth needed breaking, and asceticism was only a means of breaking such habits. Sexuality as a metaphor for the union of the Father with *Shekinah*, the Feminine Wisdom, could be a form of prayer, if a husband and wife so chose.

Asceticism, then, does not mean hatred of the body and scorn for the sexual act. In fact, given our modern lust for self-destruction, we might see the masochistic practices of our own self-indulgent era as a sort of false asceticism in which we harm the body with alcohol, cigarettes, sweets, and fat, in order to pleasure the wounded self. [Miles, *Fullness of Life*, Westminster Press, Philadelphia, 1981), p. 157] They gather up energy rather than dissipating it; they expand consciousness rather than narrowing it to mere self-indulgence; they acknowledge that the mind itself is the source of sin and that we project sin from the mind into the body, doing some fancy moral footwork as we go, rather like Adam blaming the woman for the fact that *he* ate the apple.

As man mirrors the active life of the human being in the world, so the woman, or right side of the brain, mirrors that dark, preconscious, right side in which the parts are made one. God is neither male nor female. He is the energy that marries them and puts them in step with Him. Whatever level of understanding a person may be on is the one where he or she will experience the love of God.

If a person is conscious only of a selfish level of sexuality, his sexual energy will be expressed on that level only. But if a person is aware of higher levels of being in himself, he can with conscious attention direct his sexual energies to find expression in higher levels of being as well. Professor Sherrard maintains that every individual can accomplish high degrees of control over sexual feelings and can direct creative life energies to higher levels of being. Such control of energies must be directed upwards and not allowed to revert to lower, more primitive levels.

We are all at various levels of this consciousness, this awareness of where we are in relationship to God. Our sexual feelings are a reliable barometer to our spiritual states, even though we might like to believe we are somewhere far beyond the body, resurrected before our time.

We live today in a desacralized world. Physiological acts, like sexual union, which can rightly be used as a sacrament, have been deprived of spiritual significance, and therefore of their truly human significance. If we could understand sexual union fully, in all of its infinite possibilities (as psychopathological, as a drive for power, as a biological urge, as sensual, sacred, and sacramental), we would be liberated indeed.

The mystery of sexual union reminds us that we are animals who make love, who integrate ourselves in the sex act with our opposite and with the universe as a whole.

The sense of new being and wholeness that is felt when the tension of opposites is resolved is of the greatest significance for the religious life. It is often felt as "following God's will" and is the basis of the numinous experience that comes before creeds and religions. The whole person is, then, the *contra-sexual* person in whom the male and female polarities circulate and complement each other rather than fighting and extinguishing each other. Thus we come full circle; man is seen to be created in the image of God as male and female.

Creation, as we encounter it now in our lives, represents the state after an explosion of the primal unity. The separation of the two contrary principles creates duality, suffering, and, in our Christian mythic terms, "exile from Paradise." "Paradise regained" is the result of the union of opposites, wherein the experience of duality is abolished and the phenomenal world is transcended.

It must be stated quite clearly here that this return to a man-woman state characteristic of primordial man is not to be confused with satanic hermaphroditism, as in the case of Aleister Crowley or some current movements that encourage decadent sexual practices for their own sake. These deviations are concerned not with the wholeness of man, resulting from the fusion of the sexes, but with carnal erotic diversions. The androgyne is not heterosexual, homosexual, asexual, or bisexual. He is an *arsenothelys*, "male-female," and has become transsexual in the etymological sense of the word, not in its current connotation of sex-change operations.

> Every soul and every spirt coming into this world is composed of a male and a female united in one being. Descending to earth, these two halves separate and go off to animate different bodies. At the time of marriage, the Holy One, blessed be He, Who knows all souls and spirit, unites them as before, and they become again a single body and a single soul. . . . But this union is consistent with

the actions of man and the ways he has travelled. If he is pure and behaves piously, he will enjoy a union exactly like the one that preceded his birth. [The Zohar]

The theme of mystical marriage in a religious ritual appears in the practices of the Jewish Kabbalists, who performed marital intercourse as a spiritual practice on Friday night, when the Sabbath began, and were governed by the secret life of the Godhead. Such affirmation of love between the sexes restored the union shattered by the egotism of Adam and Eve.

The reunion of God and his *Shekinah* (the Divine Glory, created nature personified as a bride) prefigures redemption. In this state, seen in purely mythical terms, the masculine and feminine are carried back to their original unity, and in this uninterrupted union of the two, the powers of generation once again flow unimpeded through all the worlds. The Kabbalists held that every religious act should be accompanied by the belief that "This is done for the sake of the reunion of God and His *Shekinah.*" [Gershom G. Scholem, *On the Kabbalah and Its Symbolism*, Schocken Books, New York, 1969]

A portion of a hymn used for the Friday evening meal says:

Her husband embraces her In her foundation, Gives her fulfilment, Squeezes out his strength.

(Foundation means the male and female organs.)

This understanding of sexual intercourse as a sacrament to aid men and women to find the supreme divine principle have overflowed into Christianity. Christian theologians, following the words of Christ, have taught that married love is the work of grace, indissoluble except by death.

Of the seven sacraments, the most frequently used by the largest section of the population is the sacrament of sex and marriage, yet a theology of sex remains to be written. Nowhere can we find an exhaustive delineation of the male-female relationship on the spiritual, psychological, and physical levels insofar as this relationship leads to God. Textbooks on the subject used in seminaries have usually been written by clerics and for clerics in defense of clerical chastity, with the intention of proving that it is the superior way of life. Sexual activities are considered, not in their potential perfection, but in regard to their possible harmful effects. The exaltation of virginity led to misogyny and, with sex, was viewed as something derived from the devil. The sacrament of sex was handed over to the secular world as a tool for advertising goods and making coarse jokes.

Biographies of saints who were once married invariably include the length of their widowhood, which purified them, or a statement that they had renounced sex during most of their marriage. The Church fought the two sources of these negative views on sex, Platonic and Manichean dualism, for centuries, but only on the doctrinal level. On the level of human life it reduced the sacrament to the duty of procreation. Even animals are not condemned to such a mechanistic state, except perhaps domestic cattle in places where artificial insemination is practiced.

But we should not be harsh with those celibates who have degraded sexual union. They had no deeper understanding of the celibate way than they did of the married way. A theology of sex must be articulated anew both for the celibate and for the married person.

The problem of opening ourselves up to the sacrament of sexual union is exactly the same as opening ourselves up to the imperishable power of grace conferred by Christ in any of the other six sacraments in the Church.

The baptized Christian has the advantage of the great mysteries, the sacraments of the mothering Church, who has taken on so much of the responsibility for her children's ascent to truth. It is not necessary for baptized Christians to repudiate their own values; rather, they should use all of their own spiritual resources and heritage, while paying due respect to the operation of divine laws within other spiritual traditions.

One of the divine laws that operates for Christians is the interaction and integration of the various sacraments. The divine law that operates universally is that of the living force of love taking possession of the inward essence of man and rescuing him from the self-assertion that is the parent of hate and division. Love, because it dissolves egotism, is the salvation of all men. Egotism not only separates man from God; it also separates him from half of humanity. It causes him to assert two mutually exclusive ideas: *I am a man* or *I am a woman*. Most spiritual traditions are concerned with transcending the ego, and have as their final goal, love and compassion for all humanity. Sexual love at its best represents love par excellence, exhibiting the type and ideal of all the other kinds of love (for example, The Song of Songs and the Letter to the Ephesians). How can we join our own lives with the new-old vision of divine love made flesh, through the flesh, in the spirit, and throughout eternity? How can we understand ourselves going into God and God coming into us through sacramental sexual union?

At the Center, we acknowledge the positive value of the God-given energies of the body, and work to draw them up from the exclusively individual genital area into the heart, from where they radiate into the whole world. To achieve this lifting of sexual energy into the heart, we develop the natural process of sublimation, which begins in adolescence, often unconsciosly. Instead of redirecting this life force into athletics, academic and aesthetic achievement, power, or the less socially acceptable outlets of aggression (hunting, fast driving, or illness), we take sexual energy directly and consciously to the altar within the heart. An ancient monastic tradition that predates Christianity called this practice *Pratyahara* and defined it: "Sense withdrawal is an exercise by which the sense organs are withdrawn from outside objects and centered in the heart."

In the technique of the consecration of sexual and creative energies into the heart, our retreatants make a very simple drawing of a geyser. Then they place a copy of the figure at eye level on a wall. Seated comfortably, they begin with scripture readings (John 4:8-26; 7:37-38), then look at the figure of the geyser and visualize it within the body. After some moments of looking at the geyser, the eyes should be closed and the remainder of the time should be spent picturing the geyser within the body. The geyser begins at the sexual center and in a powerful rush spills over into the heart. A total of thirty minutes is recommended at each sitting for this prayer practice and technique.

The lifting of sexual energy into the heart is a prayer technique that involves consciously gaining control of very dynamic and powerful life energies and thus should be done only in a prayerful and sacred context. An awareness of Christ's humanity is an essential attitude in beginning and continuing this technique, for Christ has shared fully in our human nature and He knows our nature perfectly as true man and true God. If the technique we describe is practiced as a prayer and not merely as a physical exercise, a person will succeed in giving a dynamic and energizing direction to sexuality by bringing these energies to the heart and offering them to God.

The following examples are given as the common experiences of those who begin and continue this practice. No predetermined conditon of sanctity is required, only a prayerful and loving feeling in the heart toward God and an openness to the action of the Holy Spirit within.

From the four-week journal of a twenty-eight-year-old seminarian who had given up confessing masturbation because he knew that it would happen again:

> I visualized the geyser pasted on my body, then of its own accord, it moved inside me and sprinkled water. [Later] The geyser changed into a tree with roots and waving branches. [Later] In a dream last night I was about to have a sexual affair with a person. Quickly what came to my mind was that it was wrong to do it, and the tree and geyser came into my view. [Later in relation to the symbol of the tree and the picture of the geyser] At sexual arousement or other times, like in meditation periods, the symbol of the tree comes up. Instantly the picture of the geyser appears right after and I feel the water sprinkling around my heart and chest, and there is no longer any sexual arousement, even in dreams. How very simple this is to do. Why I did not come upon it before I will never know. Also generally there is a feeling that I have conquered something big in my life. I am asking the Lord to channel this sexual energy for the love of all people.

From the journal of a fifty-year-old priest:

> I entered a light space and visualized the geyser from the genitals to the heart. I carried on a converssation with the heart: "Heart, be at peace, enjoy wholeness, open wide and be filled with this energy." I felt my heart expanding in both directions—my chest felt like it was being bound with a band. [Later] Went deep quickly. Almost immediately I felt the expansion in my heart, which later spread to just below my rib cage. During the last minutes of this sitting, I experienced a noticeable warmth around the solar plexus area. The image was of the energies flowing up the geyser into my heart and then being spilled over into the Heart of Christ and back to my own heart. During this time I experiencd my heart getting larger and larger. [Later] At Mass I found myself placing my sexual energies on the altar next to the elements of bread and wine to be sanctified with them for the Lord's love and service. [Later] I

experienced the strong desire to let all this special power of love, giving and creating, go out to others. Somewhere in this sitting I saw a huge fountain with water abundantly flowing out of its top. Afterwards I saw a huge crowd of people beneath this fountain. I found myself feeling upsurges within my heart of awe at this sheer mystery of power and love.

From the eight-week journal of a forty-two-year-old religious brother:

While doing laundry at the laundromat this morning I was surprised that women in bikinis were not sexually stimulating and something to run away from but became a beautiful handiwork of God. I was moved to pray for each one.

From the six-week journal of a twenty-three-year-old laywoman:

I am so excited about this. During the practice I got a tremendous sense of an incredible energy source that underlies everything. I became very conscious of my lower torso tingling with energy. Afterwards my face felt very warm. It gives me shivers to think about that source of immense energy. [Later] A kind of joyful warmness springing from my chest. [Later] At first when I was trying to bring the sexual energy up I was very unsuccessful. It seemed to just stay there. But finally I felt a heat move from my stomach to my heart, a warm glowing heat.

The practice of raising sexual energies is often as painful as it is joyful. One sister wrote of her experience before the icon, while consecrating her sexual energies:

The whole half-hour was nothing but an alternating *male and female sex symbol*. It was horrible and frightening. A blurred head appeared, could not really tell what it was, just a general impression it was a woman. Then an evil-looking Jack-O-Lantern came suddenly and powerfully as though he wanted to come out at me. This time I was not afraid. A Power in me commanded it to go back, and it did. It was there for most of the half hour, but much more blurred. It seemed to want to come back strongly but couldn't seem to. The ringing continues. . . .
    The pattern of sexual repression is coming out. Basically it's

a question of not accepting my own sex in myself. Jansenistic attitudes prevailed. It came across to me that sex was a necessary evil, and to be a woman meant to be dominated. The inner rebellion went on until I was about eighteen or nineteen and I went through a spiritual conversion. In the intervening years there has been spiritual and intellectual growth, but I can see the emotional crippling.

Then I asked him to bring me back to the state I was in as a baby before all adverse and contaminating influences and teachings had begun to have an influence. I had asked for a new growing awareness of the sacredness of all created things.

I spent about the first five minutes thanking God that He is restoring me to original innocence and is now showing me the way and making me realize it. Then for the breath prayer I imagined it circulating in my blood, infusing it with His energy, purifying my being. I felt a lightness and a tingling in my arms and legs, and whole body. I thanked him for this.

Then I tried to gather together all the sexual energy that is dissipated in my whole body, but especially what is now being wasted and misused, especially in my mind and heart, drew it all together into my genital area. I then imagined a corkscrew, and tried to push it (the energy) up as far as I could and asked Christ to take it from that point. I didn't stop to locate the point, but felt an upsurge in my heart, something similar to the feeling when someone takes your hands and pulls you up to the top of a wall.

My heart gave a couple of twinges, and I felt a warmth in my chest, and a light feeling in my body. I thanked Him for this. Then I felt like a child in His presence offering Him my heart and asking for His in exchange so that I can begin to love as He does. I know that He will begin to show me what this means, and I thanked Him for it.

I had scarcely begun the prayer of thanksgiving for restoration to original innocence when I felt a tingling in my arms and legs and genitalia, and a tremendous upsurge into my heart. This time the feeling was one of great force and power, yet gentleness. I thanked Him for this confirmation of the sacramental nature and holiness of sex. Then I used the same blood circulation analogy, this time specifically mentioning all my senses. Again the response was almost instantaneous, almost like the speed of blood circulation. There does not seem to be a specific pathway, but when the upsurge reaches heart level, the impression is that it comes up from behind, and falls gently and gracefully, yet with force, like an athlete doing a high jump. I did not feel any great warmth, but a deep peace.

For this woman, the consecration of her body and its powers to God was not a denial of the physical world, but an affirmation of it, a reminder of the Incarnation.

The example of the Samaritan woman at the well (John 4:5-30), who is recognized as a saint in the Ukranian Catholic Church and given a Sunday feast day, serves as a powerful illustration of what is necessary in order to "worship God in spirit and in truth." Jesus, a Jew, has asked a Samaritan to draw water for Him. Samaritans were hated enemies of the Jews and so she is shocked by his request. But Jesus replies to her: "If only you knew what God is offering and who it is that is saying to you: 'Give me a drink,' you would have been the one to ask and he would have given you living water."

This "living water" Jesus offers is different from ordinary water from a well. "Whoever drinks this water will get thirsty again; But anyone who drinks the water that I shall give will never be thirsty again: the water that I shall give will turn into a spring inside him, welling up to eternal life." It is precisely this "living water, welling up to eternal life" that we are seeking in offering to God our sexual energies for purification.

The Samaritan woman, desiring to drink of this living water, is told first to go and call her husband. After saying that she has no husband, the Lord effects her conversion by telling her everything she has ever done. He tells her that she had five husbands and that her present husband is not her own. This should not be interpreted in the literal sense, for the woman was a Samaritan, and Samaritan religious structure included belief and worship of five different religions as well as worship of the one God, Yahweh. The Samaritan woman had thus dispersed her belief among six different religions, and she is not unlike us in our displaced loyalties today. Although many Christians profess a belief in Yahweh, the true God, they do not expend full energy in prayer and service to Him; but, in the language of contemporary psychology, unrefined and misdirected sexual drives become hate, greed, lust, hunger for power, aggression, avarice, and psychosomatic forms of illness—the five "husbands" of the Samaritan woman. For those Christians who recognize these "husbands as other gods or as ways in which their creative energies are used in the service of twentieth-century forms of idolatry, the words of Christ are spoken to them: "If any man is thirsty, let him come to me! Let the man come and drink who believes in me! As Scripture says, 'From his breast shall flow fountains of living water' " (John 7:37-38).

This abandoning of twentieth-century idols can be done without the painful and discouraging efforts of renunciation by replacing the idols or husbands of misguided worship with worship and prayer to the one God. The prayerful lifting of sexual energies into the heart can lead to an inner renunciation and an inner conversion by turning toward the living waters offered to all men by Christ.

The unharnessed raw energy of a waterfall is converted into useful energy by hydroelectric power plants. From the untamed forces present in the rushing current of a waterfall comes electrical energy which can be used to illuminate lights and operate toasters and other electrical appliances. Thus a primitive form of energy is converted into useful energy and power for the service of human beings. In the same way the dynamic energies of life can be brought under control and offered to God for sanctification and use in his loving service and according to his divine will. These sanctified energies can then be directed into one's life work, into artistic endeavors, or further offered to God for use as He sees fit in completing the plan of Christian salvation.

THE CONSECRATION OF SEXUAL AND CREATIVE ENERGY INTO THE HEART

1. This exercise can be dangerous and should not be done without a competent spiritual guide. It should be done with utmost sincerity of heart.
2. Make a simple drawing of a geyser. Seated comfortably, place the drawing at eye level.
3. Place yourself in the presence of God.
4. Begin with scripture reading (John 4:8-26 or John 7:37-38), then look at the drawing of the geyser and visualize it within the body, beginning at the sexual center and spilling over into the heart.
5. After some moments of looking at the geyser, close the eyes and spend

the remainder of the time picturing the geyser within the body. Refer to the drawing of the geyser periodically if visualizing is difficult.
6. Spend thirty minutes at each practice of the exercise, doing it prayerfully and with an awareness of Christ's humanity.

CHAPTER FIVE

Work and Contemplation

> Whatever you do, do you work heartily as for the Lord rather than
> for men.
>
> Col. 3:23

Like our sexual energies, all our powers can be raised to uniting the
service of self to the service of God. The discipline of work is perhaps
the most integrating way to holiness, next to sexuality and childbearing
in its demands, rewards, and universality. Yet work, like chastity, is
thought to be a burden, an uneasy yoke which we try to escape. I myself was no different from the rest of modern people when I began my
search for the contemplative life. Perhaps even that search was a flight
from the responsibility and struggle of the physical world. If I thought
so, I soon learned that the more we are not "of the world," the more
we are "in it," one of the Lord's Zenlike paradoxes. The aim of prayer
is not escape from the ordinary life, but the transformation of that work
and that life into cocreation with God himself. It was a hard lesson for
me, as for most "liberated" modern people to learn.

Just a few weeks after I became a Catholic, Thomas Merton asked
me to go on a Zen Buddhist retreat for him and report what happened.
It was an intensive nine-day retreat with an emphasis on paying total
attention to the ordinary details of daily routines. We lived in silence,

beginning our day at 5:00 a.m. and ending at 10:00 p.m., except on the days and nights we meditated round the clock. Since the Zen Master was a Japanese who spoke little English, no talk distracted us from our total absorption in meditation and work.

I returned home, still in tears at having to leave what was, for me, the closest thing to heaven. After greeting my children, I went into the kitchen to catch up on the chaos. As I began washing the dishes and encrusted pots, it came to me that these pots and dishes were a most precious gift to me from God. He had given me these very special pots and pans; this very special stove and fridge, as a special gift of love to me. His generosity was overwhelming; I washed each dish with the care, love, and awe with which I had washed the head of my first baby when she came home from the hospital. That I loved my dirty dishes surprised me. Everyone knows that mothers love babies, but how had I missed this loving to wash dirty dishes? I had been raised to consider dishwashing and kitchen work as punishment, work suitable for servants, and certainly too far beneath me to give it any serious attention. This state of exaltation and wonder lasted for a few days while I examined each level of household operation, from basement to dining room to laundry to window-washing. I had not yet heard of Brother Lawrence or Therese of Lisieux or the Little Way.

This state of intense exaltation eventually left me; I became accustomed to experiencing joy while doing housework, but ever since that day I have never been able to use the word *work* in connection with any of my activities. I have experienced exhaustion, fatigue, even burnout, but never a moment of drudgery. It is difficult for me to try to imagine what drudgery is. Betty Freidan's insistence that women should flee the prison of their homes to work in offices leaves me completely bewildered. If you're a slave to your own demands, desires, and hatreds, you will be a slave whether you're in the home *or* the office. Not the nature of the job to be done but our attitude toward it is what makes us slave or free.

By the time we started giving retreats at the Center, we had a large amount of source material showing that in all the major religions of the world, liberation from "work" is a goal and a fairly common reality. It really broke my heart to see my children going to school and being indoctrinated into rigid, inhuman notions about what "work" is and what "play" is and being taught that they should strive to get the most money for the least "work."

The Judeo-Christian tradition has a completely different approach to our involvement with material reality—we are the hands of God in this world and we create it with Him. I went to another retreat, conducted by Merton's old friend, Rabbi Zalman Schachter, a Hasidic rabbi who used to visit Merton at Gethsemane regularly every year and make his own kind of retreat there. He helped me to understand the rich Hebraic tradition of work, which is our own birthright as Jews by adoption. In Genesis, God himself is depicted as a worker, a manual laborer, who shaped his creation as a potter shapes his clay. Like many others, I had believed that work was Adam's punishment for disobedience to God. Instead, I was taught Adam had been responsible for cultivating the Garden *before* the Fall. Not work itself, but a divided, rebellious attitude toward work was the punishment for being out of harmony with God and his divine plan for the whole cosmic order. Throughout the Talmudic tradition, rabbis urged their people to blend prayer, study, and labor. "All study of the Torah without work is futile and the cause of sin," said the great Rabbi Gamalich (Avot 2:2). His words made me remember that Our Lord himself worked as a carpenter and chose simple laborers to spread his good news that God has become incarnate in our material world, transfiguring it by his presence. I must, as Jacob Needleman wrote, "have a humility to occupy my own body" [*Lost Christianity*, Bantam Books, New York, 1980, p. 90] and to accept the consequences of being flesh as well as spirit.

Unfortunately, words like "mortification" and phrases like "dying to self" were early added to the vocabulary of Christian contemplative prayer, with connotations that stressed suffering and death rather than freedom, liberation, and unity—goals more proper to contemplation. Manichaeanism and other heresies in the early Church planted the seeds of this attitude toward prayer by rejecting the senses completely and not seeing their role in its proper perspective.

The rise of Carmelite mysticism, influenced heavily by Jewish mysticism and its unifiction of soul with body [see Appendix I on Kabbalah and *merkaba* mystics; also see pages on St. Teresa's personal background] opened the way for modern contemplatives to join prayer and work, for "Prayer cannot be accompanied by self-indulgence," as St. Teresa wrote [*The Way of Perfection*, Peers II, p. 49]. The goal of asceticism is reprogramming self-will into God's will, and no discipline can accomplish this goal so effectively as hard work, as St. Therese taught in her "Little Way." The process only *seems* painful, as does the struggle of a butterfly breaking out of its cocoon. We have found with our retreatants as they paint the window sills and feed the chickens that work undertaken as prayer is humbling, purifying, ego-chastening; all the things asceticism was meant to be at its best. When Jesus said his yoke was easy and his burden light, He meant it.

After the retreat with Rabbi Schacter, I came to the conclusion that we Christians are insufficiently educated in our own ancient tradition of work as joy. We are not educated to ask for the grace of finding our daily work anything much more than drudgery; just to find it bearable is enough for many people. The main thing we stressed in our work as contemplation was that Christ is eager to give us the grace of enjoying our work. Once people became convinced that Christ honors prayer and gives graces wherever they are asked for, there was no problem. But the deprogramming was the main part of our approach. We usually left the theological and mystical teachings of Christ washing the feet of his disciples until later when someone would announce in a group session that now they finally understood why we honor that event so much. The most difficult part of the practice was to have people examine what their motivation is in work. Whom exactly are they trying to please? A parent? A school teacher? A priest? Some other authority figure? Is work being done as a punishment? For earthly rewards? How much resentment? Joy? Like any ascetic practice, work offers us the chance to change the soul by changing the body, by breaking destructive habits and substituting radically new and constructive ones (Miles, p. 159). Once people were working to fulfill God's plan, not their own, they were peacefully tilling the Garden as Adam did before the Fall.

The journals of retreatants reflect the naturalness and simplicity of their shift into work-as-prayer, instead of work-as-punishment. After a year with us just for mending and repair, a thirty-six-year-old nun, broken and bruised, from a large, alcoholic, impoverished family, told us:

> Nothing ever happens to me in prayer like for other people, but today while I was scrubbing and peeling potatoes, Jesus was right there beside me, smiling at me, helping me peel the potatoes, which glowed like an icon. I knew I was doing the same kind of holy work that priests do at Mass with the wine and the bread. For me these potatoes were Christ's body.

Her experience was not at all uncommon. Some people came to us already quite advanced in this area. On the first day of the retreat we would ask for volunteers to do certain household and farm tasks. The person who volunteered to do the toilets, usually a priest with some parish experience, was always not only the most advanced soul, but usually the leader of the group; the one people turned to in crisis, the one who might instruct us during the retreat in some way other than Mass. This was a person who had long ago learned why Jesus washed the feet of his disciples; he knew why he was washing the feet of people about him. He was fully aware of the Church's modern reemphasis on work as a complement to prayer, on work as the fulfillment of prayer, not a distraction from it. The message of Pope John Paul II's encyclical *Laborem Exercens* is that the best motive for our work is understanding that by it we share in creation and spread the "Gospel of Work":

> We must realize that by work, even in the most ordinary activities, we share in God's creation. For, said Vatican II, in providing for themselves and their families men and women benefit society. They are unfolding the Creator's work and contributing by their industry to the realization on earth of the divine plan.

It is prayer, being in the presence of God all the time, that unites our wills with God's will and our work with God's unfolding purpose for his universe. As one of our retreatants wrote after several months at the Center:

> The feeling that comes to me lately is a deep awareness of the sacred all around me. There is no sense of drudgery or boredom in working, but a sense of divine rhythm and fullness even in the most menial tasks. Relationships with people have changed and a sense of the divine within them is very evident. Doing things for others is a pleasure, a holy joy because of a very real sense of Christ within each person. A profound sense of harmony and balance comes with this awareness. All of life, all work, all the joys and even the sorrows are infused with the divine. One gets the feeling that everything and everyone is shining and alive with the infused presence of God.

What is the common element in a prayer and work life like this man's ? What common purpose do man and God share? It is love, experienced in prayer and overflowing out of our hands into the activity of the world. Yet too often we divide prayer and work as we divide soul and body, forgetting that love is an integrative power, not a divisive one.

The world in which we live and work presents a problem to modern Christians, for we are called upon to be *in* the world and yet not *of* the world. To be half in and half out of the world is to be lukewarm in our commitments to the world and to Christ. Is it possible to be wholly for Christ and yet completely devoted to the world? Can our own work in the world become consecrated "blessed moments"? Can our union with Christ be mirrored in every activity? We can truly be in, but not of, the world by understanding our work and our quest for union with God as dynamically intertwined elements of life, not as irreconcilable opposites.

Pierre Teilhard de Chardin refers to the "two rival stars"—God and the world—that for many centuries have pulled the Christian apart and made him feel like an alien being on earth:

> Perfection consists in detachment; the world about us is vanity and ashes.
>
> The believer is constantly reading or hearing these austere words. How can he reconcile them with that other counsel, usually coming from the same master and in any case written in his heart by nature, that he must be an example unto the Gentiles in devotion to duty, in energy, and even in leadership in all the spheres opened up by man's activity"? [Enc. 108]

Teilhard says love is the solution for this dilemma:

> I would like to be able to love Christ passionately [by loving] or in the very act of loving the universe. . . . Besides communion with God and communion with the earth, is there communion with God through the earth? [Enc. 107]

Instead of seeing the material world as belonging to Satan, to be fled by prayerful Christians, Teilhard sees it as the expression of God's love. To live in it according to God's purpose, he wants us not to suffer it like a burden, but to embrace its half-formed beauty like a lover begetting a child. It is not Satan's world, but ours, given to our keeping by a loving Father. If it is sick and deformed, it is we who made it so, we who with God's help will transform it into an expression of love.

The world view predominant in traditional, harsh, ascetical spirituality was essentially static. Nothing moved; everything remained basically unchanged. Since we couldn't change the basic evil of flesh and matter, we were supposed to kill it in ourselves and become like angels. God's work of creation and Christ's act of redemption had taken place thousands of years ago, and Heaven was the only realm in which life went on. Even the view of Heaven was a static one, a place of eternal rest where the saints sat immovable in eternity, enjoying the beatific vision. Since Christ had ascended to Heaven and the work of God in creation was long ago completed, the Christian's goal was to survive the storms and temptations of this life with as few contacts with and pollutions from the world as possible, thus preserving his own soul for the glory of life beyond.

Ignace Lepp, a depth psychologist and convert to Christianity from Communism, explains this attitude of rejection of the world and of begrudgingly using the things of the world:

> The practical result of this hostility to the world is the present abyss between Christianity and the world. Happily, this hostility to the world as we have described it has nothing to do with the essence of Christianity. The terrestrial and the natural are the work of God and the object of His love.

The mode of activity in traditional spirituality was a static one as well. The work of each person was of little importance; the only value lay in directing the intention behind the work toward God. Thus a person developed an attitude of working for God as a servant or employee. But the work itself did not matter; only the thought behind the work gave meaning to it. Any activity held an inferior place to the purity of the intention with which it was done.

Teilhard helped to renew the notion that work itself, the very activities which occupy us, are redeemable. The divinization of our endeavor by the value of the intention put into it, pours a priceless soul into all our actions, but it does not confer the hope of resurrection upon human bodies. Yet that hope is what we need if our joy is to be complete.

It is certainly a great thing to be able to think that if we love God, something of our inner activity will never be lost. But will not the work itself, of our minds, of our hearts, and of our hands, that is to say, our achievements, our products, our opus—will not this, too, in some sense, be "eternalized" and saved?

To work and to value the intention, occupies us in working for God. To work and to realize that our work is meaningful in God's plan here and now, makes us workers with God, as St. Paul wrote: "We are fellow workers with God . . ." (1 Cor. 3:9).

To work in cooperation with God is to review the nature of creation, not as a static, one-time occurrence, but as a dynamic, transforming process that is continually evolving and growing to perfection. It is to view the cross in our lives as the promise and the gate to life; to see the world as the dynamic milieu of our sanctification and the sanctification of others; and to see not only our intention, but the very acts of our labor as cooperative creation with God toward building a new heaven and a new earth.

Modern science, especially physical science, reveals more and more that matter and life are not static phenomena, but in constant motion. New things are constantly happening, change takes place around us with incomprehensible speed, and creation continues to operate in each moment, in every cell and every atom of our varied and marvelous universe.

Vatican II acknowledged this pattern of constant growth and change and recognized a new age of man that the increase in scientific discovery has prepared:

> The circumstances of the life of modern man have been so profoundly changed in their social and cultural aspects that we can speak of a new age of human history. New ways are open, therefore, for the perfection and the further extension of culture. These ways have been prepared by the enormous growth of natural, human and social sciences, by technical progress, and advances in developing and organizing means whereby men can communicate with one another. [CMW II, 1, #54]

The new age is one of evolution and involvement. It calls for a renewal of spiritualities formerly based upon an isolated Christian in a static world. It seeks a redefinition of work that is in accord with the spirit of growth, evolution, and transformation.

In *Homo Ludens: A Study of the Play Element in Culture,* Johan Huizinga wrote that play was essentially creative, being voluntary, sacred, and disinterested. The same qualities are obvious in contemplative prayer and work. Contemplative work, work that is prayer, is at the heart of creeative activity and is completely freed from drudgery, boredom, and monotony. At the Center, many retreatants found that what was formerly play is now hard work, or boring drudgery, while prayer and physical labor have become joyful, even playful, activity. As one of our retreatants wrote:

> I was working all morning, refinishing a large cedar chest. While I was working, I was very aware of my work as prayer. All of a sudden the chest rose up in front of my eyes. It became so sacred and holy that I had to bless it. The chest became to me an altar and I felt as if I was at Mass. At the end of the work, I went to wash up at the sink and, it, too, rose up and became so sacred I had to bless it. As I was washing the dishes one night, the whole atmosphere—everything around me—became sacred, the sink, the soapy water, the glasses, plates, pots, and pans were all holy. I began to bless everything and everyone in sight.

Objects once seen as dull become charged with the same spirit of God that illumines and transforms the heart in prayer.

Play interrupts the appetitive process and stands as a temporary activity, satisfying in and of itself. This characteristic of the disinterestedness of play is also a description of "renouncing the fruits of one's labor." Sacred work can also be said to be "a temporary activity satisfying in itself and ending there." Detachment from the fruits of one's labor is a key to understanding work as cocreation, as sanctified activity in the presence of and with the cooperation of God.

Much of twentieth-century activity is based upon the fruits of our labor—the salary, the paid vacation, and the fringe benefits are what seemingly motivate many people to work. Yet, as long as one bases the motivation for work on the fruits of the work, or avoids work because of the bitter fruits, then he is enslaved to desire and will never escape disappointments and rigors in working. To act and not to seek the fruits is to act for the sake of the action itself; and the work itself becomes the fruit; the reward is inherent in the work being done. All the more so, if "the heart of the worker is fixed on the highest." This fixing of the heart on God is the essence of contemplative activity and is the source of our participation with God in continuing the act of creation. The culmination of our work at the Center was not, then, the bliss of a contemplative experience, a "rapture," but spreading the radiance of God's love beyond the individual's prayer life.

Well along in our retreats, when people were getting close to being convinced that there can be spiritual joy in "work," we would assign simple tasks to be accompanied by their breath prayer—for instance, the folding of cards, the sorting of a box of nuts and bolts into two separate piles, the washing of dinner dishes. At the end of the day, retreatants would simply enter in their journals how much of the time they were able to use their breath prayer while working. From the journal of a priest:

> Am typing addresses on envelopes. Breath prayer twice before each one. After name is typed I sent out a "beam" of Heart Blessing to the Party and then typed the street and city. [Later] Cut boughs for flower boxes and placed them in boxes in front of windows. I found out again how easy it can be to start thinking of the details of the job or its relevancy instead of keeping it a contemplative experience. I'll have to watch myself better.

As this man understood, work *outside* must be joined to work *inside*; the process is the same, and so is the goal.

The second week, we would assign more complex problem-solving work, such as folding a card and pasting on a picture, or filling orders for the cards. All the while, they began with the prayer of consecration and asked for God's grace to experience cocreation with Him. By the third week, we had people at their tasks, not necessarily with their breath prayer, but with a miniature icon, practicing the prayer of loving regard. When they were able to sustain some level of contemplative prayer while the mental operation of their assigned "work" was going on, they were ready for reentry into their life.

Usually reentry was on the last week of the four-week retreat. We simply asked the retreatant to duplicate one hour of whatever kind of "work" they were going to return to, and have them do it accompanied by the prayer of loving regard or the breath prayer, whichever seemed easier. Many of our retreatants were teachers in some capacity, and many learned to conduct their classes or write out lectures with the icon in front of them for months, even years, after they returned to their jobs and homes.

Another part of the reentry program was to run the lawnmower outside the chapel window at prayer time, play secular rock music near the chapel, and borrow some neighbor children to play a noisy game. The racket was irritating to the retreatants at first, after three weeks of rural, bucolic quiet, with only singing birds to distract them. In a couple of days, however, they would usually overcome the distraction and feel more secure about being able to continue their prayer practices back home.

On what psychological evidence do we base our effort to integrate work and prayer? Since "split-brain" research made clear a division in brain function, concentrating analytical work in the left hemisphere and synthesizing, intuitive work in the right, we have been aware that our culture overemphasizes intellect to the detriment of emotion and intuition. No wonder we reward and honor the scientist, while despising manual laborers.

Harmony exists in life when one can have a balance between the two hemispheres and be freed of the tyranny of exclusive left-hemisphere dominance. Recent experiments in education have tried to integrate rather than divide our activity, and develop the right brain to increase creative ability. We attempt a similar development of the right brain, encouraging a nonintellectual awareness of a whole action. As people "pray their work," they pay less attention to verbalizing and analyzing a task than to losing themselves in it, becoming part of it, feeling its relationship to the flow of life around them. Fearing that people might be alarmed at the use of a modern "gimmick" in their prayer, we waited until someone would report progress in work as prayer; then we would explain the mental process involved.

Also, with the hope of quieting the strident left brain, we ask people at the Center to do their spiritual reading before they arrive. (Their bibliography is provided in Appendix X of this book.) Only the Scriptures are read during the retreat—read, but not studied. We ask people simply to look at the words with attention and openness, absorbing the message under the words as our bodies use the invisible vitamins in the food we eat. Such reading for inspiration and contemplation ideally takes place in the language centers of the right brain, which are not devoted to decoding and judging, but to feeling. The Scriptures are thus absorbed by the heart, not grasped by the brain. This exercise in awareness, like many others practiced at the Center, deepens the retreatants' capacity for using the right hemisphere in their work.

As prayer spreads through a larger and larger area of daily activity, the right brain is apparently brought more and more into prominence. This shift away from the divisive intellect toward the heart helps us to understand, in part, what mystics meant when they spoke of "dying to the self" and "growth into God." The following simple, nontechnical schema is offered to retreatants well into their work practice so that they will understand the theory behind what they do:

Left Hemisphere	Right Hemisphere
analytical, logical	intuitive
verbal	symbolic
mathematical	creative, artistic
active	passive, receptive
finite	infinite
comprehends	apprehends
linear time	timelessness
biological survival	spiritual center
self-love	parapsychological
self-will	divine element
memory, imagination, will	space orientation
sex as biological	sex as sacrament
cultural conditioning	man's true nature
false-self (ego)	

Most people in our culture are left-hemisphere developed, even over-developed. We reward achievements in the left hemisphere functions, and in some cases, we even punish children for being primarily right-brained. From the list, it is clear that many of the actions we call sinful spring from excesses in the left hemisphere, as do most of the obstacles. In the prayer process, when we leave the *kataphatic* verbal prayers and go into *apophatic*, or nonverbal contemplative prayer, we see a rapid development in right-hemisphere functions. They, in turn, aid prayer and move the person to direct experience of God, instead of simply knowledge about God. The person discovers more and more deeply that he is created in the image and likeness of God. God is *known*, not just *known about*.

Thus we have examined a way of praying without ceasing, involving the whole body, the whole mind, and the whole strength. The breath prayer frees the mind from the tyranny of thoughts directed to things other than God; the heart is purified and nourished by direct Christ-love; the creative energies are redirected to their maker for further instruction and use by the consecration of creative energies prayer. The brain is partially restored and redirected through the icon practice and the prayer of loving regard. The whole body is rededicated to Christ for his ministry through work as contemplation. Far from being a flight from the world, we see that contemplation is a flight into it. One retreatant wrote:

> A feeling of being a winged white stallion flying into the sun; of absolute union with grass and flowers; an unbreakable soldering with all persons of all races and places; of being one with the mineral bowels of the earth; of greatest humility combined with greatest exaltation in God's loving care; of being all things since the beginning of time, in all things animate, and inanimate, out of time and space, yet intimately bound with every breath of every creature.

The world around us is sacred, holy, a place filled with the Spirit of God that gives it life. To reject or deny the world is to negate the Spirit; to accept and joyfully embrace the world is to affirm the Spirit that gives it life. Our activity, our work in the world, can be God's work, in union with the Spirit that fills all things.

> As the hand held before the eyes hides the tallest mountain, so this small earthly life hides from our gaze the vast radiance and secrets of which the world is full, and whoever can take life from before his eyes, as one takes away one's hand, will see the great radiance within the world. [Martin Buber, *Ten Rungs: Hasidic Sayings*, Schocken Books, New York, 1947, pp. 38, 53, 60.

Last Thoughts

I can now confess that most of what you have read thus far has been written with the greatest restraint. The reason for this is that what I really have to say can be summed up in one sentence: Let God love you.

Say yes to his insatiable craving to fill you, transform you, engulf and absorb you in his endless, passionate, insane love. God's love is completely without reason. It is like the love of a young child who has been mutilated by a battering mother, taken to a hospital, bound up, caressed, then asked by the social worker, "Where would you like to live?" The child answers, "With my mother." Is that a reasonable love?

Apparently no matter how we insult, offend, or mutilate God, his children, or his creation, He still wants to live with us. He forgives so readily in his craving for our love that it seems like madness. If a wife were to repeatedly forgive her husband for beating her and her children, she would be taken to a psychiatric treatment center and labeled a psychopathic personality for permitting such treatment in the name of "love."

Yet God is like that beaten child or battered wife in his irrational love for us. His craving for us seems like the obsession of an insane person. He cannot give us enough love to satisfy himself. Furthermore, He can never get enough of our love either. There is no way that human beings can place themselves beyond God's redeeming love. There is no crime, no sin, that can permanently close the door. With only the slightest inclination of our heart towards him in contrition and appeal, He is there, pouring out his bottomless, endless love to us. Unlike battered humans, He can never stop himself from forgiving us and giving us yet another chance to become his beloved.

The truth of this book and all the practices it contains is that they are not really necessary at all, but are a waste of time unless we say one word: "YES!"

YES to God's passionate, senseless, indiscriminate love.

YES to all the endless gifts that his senseless and indiscriminate love has designed for us.

YES to his easy forgiving and his forgetfulness of our spiritual temper tantrums, our pride, our contempt and hate, our violation of his family and his home.

YES to his promises of heaven on earth.

YES to his eternal fidelity to us in spite of all we do to test and destroy it.

YES to making us divine with Him, to sitting and reigning with Him in his kingdom.

YES to being his bride.

Ezekiel

INTRODUCTION

In the thirtieth year, on the fifth day of the fourth month, as I was among the exiles on the bank of the river Chebar, heaven opened and I saw visions from God. On the fifth of the month—it was the fifth year of exile for King Johoiachin—the word of Yahweh was addressed to the priest Ezekiel, son of Buzi, in the land of the Chaldaeans, on the bank of the river Chebar.

THE VISION OF THE "CHARIOT OF YAHWEH"

There the hand of Yahweh came on me. I looked; a stormy wind blew from the north, a great cloud of light around it, a fire from which flashes of lightning darted, and in the center a sheen like bronze at the heart of the fire. In the center I saw what seemed four animals. They looked like this. They were of human form. Each had four faces. Each had four wings. Their legs were straight, they had hooves like oxen, glittering like polished brass. Human hands showed under their wings; the faces of all four were turned to the four quarters. Their wings touched each other; they did not turn as they moved; each one went straight forward.

As to what they looked like, they had human faces, and all four had a lion's face to the right, and all four had a bull's face to the left, and all four had an eagle's face. Their wings were spread upwards; each had two wings that touched, and two wings that covered his body; and they all went straight forward; they went where the spirit urged them; they did not turn as they moved.

Between these animals something could be seen like flaming brands or torches, darting between the animals; the fire flashed light, and lightning streaked from the fire. And the creatures ran to and fro like thunderbolts.

I looked at the animals; there was a wheel on the ground by each of them, one beside each of the four. The wheels glittered as if made of chrysolite. All four looked alike, and seemed to be made one inside the other. They went forward four ways and kept their courses unswervingly. Their rims seemed enormous when I looked at them and all four rims had eyes all the way around. When the animals went forward, the wheels went forward beside them; and when the animals left the ground, the wheels too left the ground. Where the spirit urged them, there the wheels went, since the spirit of the animal was in the wheels. When the animals moved on, they moved on; when the former halted, the latter halted; when the former left the ground, the wheels too left the ground, since the spirit of the animal was in the wheels. Over the heads of the animals, a sort of vault, gleaming like crystal, arched above their heads; under this vault their wings stretched out to one another, and each had two covering his body. I heard the noise of the wings as they moved; it sounded like rushing water, like the voice of Shaddai, a noise like a storm, like the noise of a camp; when they halted, they folded their wings, and there was a noise.

Above the vault over their heads was something that looked like a sapphire; it was shaped like a throne and high up on this throne was a being that looked like a man. I saw him shine like bronze, and close to and all around him, from what seemed his loins upwards, was what looked like fire; and from what seemed his loins downwards I saw what looked like fire, and a light all around like a bow in the clouds on rainy days; that is how the surrounding light appeared. It was something that looked like the glory of Yahweh. I looked, and prostrated myself, and I heard a voice speaking.

THE VISION OF THE SCROLL

It said, "Son of man, stand up; I am going to speak to you." As he said these words, the spirit came into me and made me stand up, and I heard him speaking to me. He said, "Son of man, I am sending you to the Israelites, to the rebels who have turned against me. Till now they and their ancestors have been in revolt against me. The sons are defiant and obstinate; I am sending you to them, to say, "The Lord Yahweh says this." Whether they listen or not, this set of rebels shall know there is a prophet among them. And you, son of man, do not be afraid of them, do not be afraid when they say, "There are thorns all around you and scorpions under you." There is no need to be afraid either of their words or of their looks, for they are a set of rebels. You must deliver my words to them whether they listen or not, for they are a set of rebels.

"You, son of man, listen to the words I say; do not be a rebel like that rebellious set. Open your mouth and eat what I am about to give you." I looked. A hand was there, stretching out to me and holding a scroll. He unrolled it in front of me; it was written on back and front; on it was written lamentations, wailings, moanings. He said, "Son of man, eat what is given to you; eat this scroll, then go and speak to the House of Israel." I opened my mouth; he gave me the scroll to eat and said, "Son of man, feed and be satisfied by the scroll I am giving you." I ate it, and it tasted sweet as honey.

Ezekiel 1:1-28; 2:1-9; 3:1-3

The Christian Kabbalah*

From the late fifteenth century onward, in certain Christian circles of a mystical and theosophical persuasion a movement began to evolve with the object of harmonizing kabbalistic doctrines with Christianity, and, above all, of demonstrating that the true, hidden meaning of the teachings of the Kabbalah points in a Christian direction. Naturally, such views did not meet with a friendly reception from the kabbalists themselves, who expressed nothing but derision for the misunderstandings and distortions of kabbalistic doctrine of which Christian Kabbalah was full; but the latter undeniably succeeded in arousing lively interest and debate among spiritualistic circles in the West until at least the middle of the eighteeneth century. Historically, Christian Kabbalah sprang from two sources. The first was the christological speculations of a number of Jewish converts who are know to us from the end of the thirteenth century until the period of the Spanish expulsion [G. Scholem, in *Essays Presented to Leo Baeck*, 1954, pp. 158-93, such as "Abner of Burgos (Yizhak Baer, Tarbiz 27, 1958, pp. 152-63), and Paul de Heredia, who pseudoepigraphically composed several texts of Christian Kabbalah entitled *Iggeret ha-Sodot* and *Galei Rezaya* in the name of Judah ha-Nasi and other tannaim.

Another such tract put out by Jewish converts in Spain toward the end of the fifteenth century, and written in imitation of the styles of the aggadah and the Zohar, circulated widely in Italy. Such compositions had little effect on serious Christian spiritualists, nor was their clearly tendentious missionary purpose calculated to win readers. Another matter entirely, however, was the Christian speculation about the Kabbalah that first developed around the Platonic Academy endowed by the Medicis in Florence and pursued in close connection with the new horizons opened up by the Renaissance in general. These Florentine circles believed that they had discovered in the Kabbalah an original divine revelation to mankind that had been lost and would now be restored. With the help of this revelation, they believed it was possible not only to understand the teachings of Pythagoras, Plato, and the Orphics, all of whom they greatly admired, but also the secrets of the Catholic faith. The founder of this Christian school of Kabbalah was the renowned Florentine prodigy Giovanni Pico della Mirandola (1463-94), who had long passages of kabbalistic literature translated for him into Latin by the very learned convert Raymond Moncada, also known as Flavious Mithridates. Pico began his kabbalistic studies in 1486, and when he displayed his 900 famous theses for public debate in Rome, he included among them forty-seven propositions taken directly from kabbalistic sources, the majority from Recanati's commentary on the Torah and seventy-two more propositions that represented his own conclusions from his kabbalistic research.

These theses, especially the daring claim that "no science can better convince us of the divinity of Jesus Christ than magic and the Kabbalah," first brought the Kabbalah to the attention of many Christians. The ecclesiastical authorities fiercely rejected this and other of Pico's propositions, and there ensued the first real debate on the subject of the Kabbalah ever to take place in humanistic and clerical circles. Pico himself believed that he could prove the dogmas of the Trinity and the Incarnation on the basis of kabbalistic axioms. The sudden discovery of an esoteric Jewish tradition that had hitherto been completely unknown caused a sensation in the Christian intellectual world, and Pico's subsequent writings on the Kabbalah helped to further increase the interest of Christian Platonists in these newly uncovered sources, particularly in Italy, Germany, and France. Under Pico's influence the great Christian Hebraist Johannes Reuchlin (1455-1522) also took up the study of Kabbalah and published two Latin books on the subject, the first ever to be written by a non-Jew, *De Verbo Mirifico* [*On the Miracle-working*

Name, 1494] and *De Arte Cabalistica* [*On the Science of the Kabbalah*, 1517].

The years between these two dates also witnessed the appearance of a number of works by the learned convert Paul Ricius, the private physician of Emperor Maximilian, who took Pico's and Reuchlin's conclusions and added to them through an original synthesis of kabbalistic and Christian sources. Reuchlin's own main contribution was his association of the dogma of the Incarnation with a series of bold speculations on the kabbalistic doctrine of the Divine Names of God. Human history, Reuchlin argued, could be divided into three periods. In the first or natural period, God revealed himself to the patriarchs through the three-lettered name of *Shaddai*. In the period of the Torah He revealed himself to Moses through the four-lettered name of the *Tetragrammaton*. But in the period of grace and redemption He revealed himself through five letters, namely, the *Tetragrammaton*, with the addition of the letter *shin*, signifying the Logos, thus spelling Yehoshua or Jesus. In the name of Jesus, which is the true Miraculous Name, the formerly forbidden name of God now became pronounceable. In Reuchlin's schematic arrangement, which was able to draw for support on the common abbreviation for Jesus in medieval manuscripts, JHS, Jewish beliefs in three world ages (Chaos, Torah, Messiah) blended with the tripartite Christian division of the millennialist school of Joachim of Fiore into a reign of the Father, a reign of the Son, and a reign of the Holy Spirit.

Pico's and Reuchlin's writings, which place the Kabbalah in the context of some of the leading intellectual developments of the time, attracted wide attention. They led on the one hand to considerable interest in the doctrine of Divine Names and in practical Kabbalah, and on the other hand to further speculative attempts to achieve a synthesis between kabbalistic motifs and Christian theology. The place of honor accorded to practical Kabbalah in Cornelius Agrippa of Nettesheim's great compendium, *De Occulta Philosphia* (1531), which was a widely read summary of all the occult sciences of the day, was largely responsible for the mistaken association of the Kabbalah in the Christian world with numerology and witchcraft. Several Christian kabbalists of the mid-sixteenth century made a considerable effort to master the sources of the Kabbalah more deeply, both in Hebrew and in Latin translations prepared for them, thus widening the basis for their attempts to discover common ground between the Kabbalah and Christianity. Among the most prominent of these figures were Cardinal Egidio da Viterbo (1465-1532), whose *Scechina* (edited by F. Secret, 1959) and *On the Hebrew Letters* were influenced by ideas in the Zohar and the Sefer ha-Temunah, and the Franciscan Francesco Giorgio of Venice (1460-1540), the author of two large and at the time widely read books, *De Harmonia Mundi* (1525) and *Problemata* (1536), in which the Kabbalah assumed a central place and manuscript material from the Zohar was used extensively for the first time in a Christian work. The admiration of these Christian authors for the Kabbalah aroused an angry reaction in some quarters, which accused them of disseminating the view that any Jewish kabbalist could boast of being a better Christian than an orthodox Catholic. A more original mystical thinker who was also better acquainted with the Jewish sources was the renowed Frenchman Guillaume Postel (1510-1581), one of the outstanding personalities of the Renaissance. Postel translated the Zohar and the Sefer Yezirah into Latin even before they had been printed in the original, and accompanied his translation with a lengthy theosophic exposition of his own views. In 1548 he published a kabbalistic commentary in Latin translation on the mystical significance of the menorah, and later a Hebrew edition as well. These authors had many connections in Jewish circles.

During this period, Christian Kabbalah was primarily concerned with the development of certain religious and philosophical ideas for their own sake rather than with the desire to evangelize among Jews, though this latter activity was occasionally stressed to justify a pursuit that was otherwise suspect in many eyes. One of the most dedicated of such Christian kabbalists was Johann Albrecht Widmanstetter (Widmanstadius; 1506-1557), whose enthusiasm for the Kabbalah led him to collect many kabbalistic manuscripts that are extant in Munich. Many of his contemporaries, however, remained content to speculate in the realm of Christian Kabbalah without any firsthand knowledge of the sources. Indeed, in the course of time, the knowledge of Jewish sources diminished among the Christian kabbalists, and consequently the Jewish element in their books became progressively slighter, its place being taken by esoteric Christian speculations whose connections with Jewish motifs were remote. The Lurianic revival in Safed had no effect on these circles. Their commitment to missionary work increased, yet the number of Jewish converts to Christianity from kabbalistic motives, or of those who claimed such motives retrospectively, remained disproportionately small among the numbers of converts in general. There is no clear evidence in the writings of such Christian theosophists to indicate whether or not they believed the Jewish kabbalists to be hidden or unconscious Christians at heart. In any event, Christian Kabbalah occupied an honored place both in the sixteenth century, primarily in Italy and France, and in the seventeenth century, when its center moved to Germany and England.

In the seventeenth century Christian Kabbalah received two great impetuses, one being the theosophical writings of Jacob Boehme, and the other Christian Knorr von Rosenroth's vast kabbalistic compendium, *Kabbala Denudata* (1677-84), which for the first time made available to interested Christian readers, most of whom were undoubtedly mystically inclined themselves, not only important sections of the Zohar but sizable excerpts from Lurianic Kabbalah as well. In this work and in the writings of the Jesuit scholar Athanasius Kircher, the parallel is drawn for the first time between the kabbalistic doctrine of Adam Kadmon and the concept of Jesus as primordial man in Christian theology. This analogy is pressed particularly in the essay entitled *"Adumbratio Kabbalae Christianae"*, which appears at the end of the *Kabbala Denudata* (Fr. trans., Paris, 1899). Its anonymous author was in fact the well-known Dutch theosophist, Franciscus Mercurious van Helmont, all of whose works are shot through with kabbalistic ideas. It was Van Helmont who served as the link between the Kabbalah and the Cambridge Platonists led by Henry More and Ralph Cudworth, who made use of kabbalistic motifs for their own original speculative purposes (More especially). Somewhat earlier, students (as well as opponents) of Jacob Boehme had discovered the inner affinity between his own theosophical system and that of the Kabbalah, though there would seem to be no historical connection between them, and in certain circles, particularly in Germany, Holland, and England, Christian Kabbalah henceforward assumed a Boehmian guise. In 1673 a large chart was erected in front of a Protestant church in Teinach (in southern Germany), which had as its purpose the presentation of a kind of visual summary of this school of Christian Kabbalah. Several different interpretations were given to it.

As early as the late sixteenth century a pronounced trend had emerged toward the permeation of Christian Kabbalah with alchemical symbolism, thus giving it an oddly original character in its final stages of development in the seventeenth and eighteenth centuries. This melange of elements typifies the works of Heinrich Khunrath [*Amphitheatrum Sapientiae Aeternae*, 1609], Blaise de Vigenere [*Triaite du feu*, 1617], Abraham von Frankenberg and Robert Fludd (1547-1637), and Thomas Vaughan (1622-1666), and reaches its apogee in Georg von Wellling's *Opus Mago-Cabbalisticum* (1735) and the many books of F.C. Oetinger (1702-1782), whose influence is discernible in the works of such great figures of German idealist philosophy as Hegel and Schelling. In yet another form this mixture reappears in the theosophical systems of the Freemasons in the second half of the eighteenth century. A late phase of Christian Kabbalah is represented by Martines de Pasqually (1727-1774) in his *Traite de la reintegration des etres*, which greatly influenced theosophical currents in France. The author's disciple was the well-known mystic Louis Claude de St. Martin. Pasqually himself was suspected during his lifetime of being a secret Jew, and modern scholarship has in fact established that he was of Marrano ancestry. The sources of his intellectual indebtedness, however, have still to be clarified. The crowning and final achievement of Christian Kabbalah was Franz Josef Molitor's comprehensive *Philosophie der Geschichte oder Ueber die Tradition* (1779-1861), which combined profound speculation in a Christian kabbalistic vein with suggestive research into the ideas of the Kabbalah itself. Molitor, too, still clung to a fundamentally christological view of the Kabbalah, whose historical evolution he completely failed to understand, yet at the same time he revealed an essential grasp of kabbalistic doctrine and in insight into the world of the Kabbalah far superior to that of most Jewish scholars of his time.

* "The Christian Kabbalah" in *The Encyclopedia Judaica*, vol. 10, Keter Publishing House, Jerusalem, Israel, 1971, pp. 643-646.

The Prayer of Loving Regard

From the journal of a fifty-year-old priest (Father John):

Second sitting with icon:

More light—icon becoming three-dimensional like a brilliant diamond flashing.

Later—much more golden—image of beautiful sea-horse, also a tiger and a peacock with little star on top of head.

Later—icon appears to be huge female breast.

Later—soft green, blue, red and gray—many miniature pictures—crowned head of Christ; the head of an ape—a skull—picture of Hitler—a triangle—a square or rectangle beautifully done in form of etching.

Later—icon—very bright flashing yellow light at borders, changed to soft white—center became an eye staring at me—a babbling baboon—chattering away. . .very disturbing—female breast.

Later—(while walking)—very pleasing perfume coming from earth.

Later—icon—embracing couples—very tenderly embracing—graceful dancing couples—ballet, waltz—some letters appeared clearly—G.T. and Y.—a beautiful five-pointed star. A very seductive eye—a woman holding her breast like madonna. Flowers—a single lily and a rose—very pleasant experience.

From the journal of a thirty-five-year-old graduate student Michael M.:

First fifteen-minute sitting:

The icon was lost a number of times...Icon appeared as window, looking into a depth beyond space and time...light at end of tunnel.

Second sitting:

...A terrible beauty is born...lots and lots of light, above, around and below...pulsating bright and dull...I tried to breathe in the light...time went fast...It appeared as if the icon was a cover under which the beautiful warm light is pressing to escape . . .

Later:

...I have a feeling that a great deal is a-borning in me...I felt peace and a great deal of love for all.

Fifth day:

The light from behind the icon is reaching almost to ceiling....
I haven't taken dope in years, but the only way of describing my consciousness of the events is a high experience. Beautiful.... All the highs I looked for in booze and dope have always been within me, for it was Jesus who has given me the opportunity to open my inner eyes to see Him on the altar. Thank you, Lord. Could I sit at icon thirty minutes prior to liturgy?

Later:

In liturgy, the light was often present over altar, especially when John read from Gospel...my experience of the sacrifice being out of time and space, occurring NOW, not 2000 years ago.

Later:

The light is growing more intense, pulsating from the source.

Later:

...black or dark birds, geese, rising from no particular level upward.

...during the day I am experiencing a great deal of clarity of thought, nothing specific, just cleanliness of the head.

...experienced some sensation in heart-area which I can't express verbally yet.

...the center dot, splitting into two and moving around...suddently coincided and reduced to a single pinpoint of blue-gold light. Very brilliant...my eyes felt its heat. It felt like a presence...it felt reverent.

Later:

Wanted to see dot of light again but did not.

Later:

A triangle appeared in center. Then pinpoint of bright light—very beautiful.

Later:

Again expereinced blue-gold brilliant light.

Later:

A blue flame surrounded the intense pinpoint of light. The source of light, energy, matter, the world. Heavy! Quite happy.

Later:

Too tired to concentrate—nothing going on—a low profile day for me. (Note by retreat director: Possibly integrating experience?)

Later:

I feel a joy, an abandonment of self and trust of self in dedication to Christ. This is something different than before.

Later:

Could have sworn I heard some ringing in left ear at end of sitting.

Later:

. . .the light is no longer blue with gold. . .but blue, intense like lightening. Everything had gone black. the light went to gold with a bright light within it. All of a sudden it was awe, not fear.

At the Liturgy:

A high experience, especially when I read the Word of the Lord. It resonated deep within my being, especially my heart. . .a glow, a high, a fullnes..

Later:

As soon as I begin to think about the light, its beauty, its intensity, its meaning, it goes away. . .awoke at night with a warm glow in my heart, saying my breath prayer. . .burning sensation in heart when doing consecration of sexual energy. . .so much light. . .staggering. . . overwhelming.

Later:

Headache—bad sitting.

(Note: Another period of integration)

Later:

. . .definite warmth and glow in heart. . .His flow of love into my heart like a blue fog rolling in and caressing my heart, or a gentle wave, very tender and loving.

Later:

I just contemplate the dazzling light. If it were physical light I'd have to wear welder's glasses, it's so bright.

Later:

Tingling and numbness, slight disorientation in space, something quite different from any drug or alcoholic experience—very pretty.

Later:

...constant heart warmth in sitting—much tranquility and peace, yet alert and energetic. Mental feeling of cleanliness, purity, and elation...blinding light in the Radiant Heart-to-Heart picture....

Later (after healing of memories):

I really have the feeling "I know something you don't know" that kids play. Only I don't really know what I do have. Yet I know it's something I want everyone to know, to share it. But the ramifications are staggering and I'm not really ready to think of them . . .

...heart warmth all day long now, great happiness within....

the heart is going dark...the darkness is bright...I felt very vulnerable—all my defenses down—exposed...whining noise in my head like a giant turbine....

...flash of brilliance like hot, bright sun...sound of birds humming in my head....

...the dark brightness seems deeper than the brightness...the bright-darkness is like a rare, precious stone....

seeing light throughout entire mass...reading Scripture—the pages scream out "LOVE"....

The Healing of Memories

A typical series of responses—from the journal of a forty-year-old priest:

I was surprised at how many hurts and resentments are in me over the nineteen months; I prayed to be set free from these and not be held captive by them. I prayed that others whom I had affected by my resentment and sins be set free also.

(Note: This surprise is typical of someone who has gone to confession regularly.)

Later:

Before I went to 1974-76, I thought again of the last two years and tried to make sure there was no bitterness left toward those who hurt me. Instead, I saw those hurts as integral to God's plan to bring me where I am now. In the 1974-76 period I found several hurts I had not forgiven that were still very real; I offered these to Jesus' power in the host as sacrifices of my own life.

Later:

I found several deep wounds in the time I covered last night (1974-76), things I had not really forgiven. I placed them in the fire of Jesus' heart furnace to burn them, then offered my wounded self to Jesus in the Eucharist to be healed.

Later:

I dwelt upon a very painful time of my life, the first six months of 1970 and saw that so much of what happened in those eight years flowed from the hurts of that time. I allowed Jesus to touch, heal, restore, and renew me, then rested in his presence.

Later:

Considered the time 1963-66 but I got a tremendous headache that would not go away. It lasted till after midnight (I never get headaches). I prayed for healing and touched my head with my hands. Nothing. I took medicine. Nothing. During my hour of vigil I realized that if the Lord had not healed me, it was his permissive will. . . .

(Peter's entry in the journal at this point: Your resistances cannot be blamed on God and does not require His healing, but your surrender.)

Later:

Went over the years 1956-59. Only a few hurts there but some deeper than I thought. Offered all these to Jesus for His healing.

Later:

1950-56. Certain things surfaced almost immediately. Things I had not thought of in years.

(Note: Typical of unexpected recall of forgotten memories of twenty years ago.)

Later:

Tears, or rather, sobbing poured out of me. All the rejections and hurts I have experienced in all my life came before me and I wept in my desolation. Pent-up tears. Freeing tears. Healing tears. Then the word of God within me very clearly: "I know you. I love you. I am with you as I have been every step of your life." Tears of gratitude, unbelief, yet total conviction of this tremendous love.

Later:

After our conversation, I wept profusely. I don't know what's happening through all this, but there is a sense of hell almost about it—the concentration of feelings (of intensity) concerning rejection, pain, loneliness, valuelessness, and the burden of being "different" is so obviously "packed in"—as though a whole lifetime of feelings were hitting me at one time. This is frightening. Is it also a purification, a healing and a prelude to deeper knowledge of God's love, acceptance and compassionate tenderness? God as my gentle, embracing Father, Jesus as sensitive, all-giving lover? I spent until 11:30 sitting in my room because I was still crying and felt totally energyless, unable to push myself beyond this particular moment of pain and a need to just let it happen.

I feel drained still.

(Peter's answer in the journal:)

Most apt description. Satan does work through our natural weaknesses, especially strongly as we are making great strides spiritually, as you have been this month. Satan, in combination with one's tendencies, can bring us to despondency, to despair, to reject the grace and healing of what God has given us; say, with Jesus: "Get thee behind me, Satan, the power and grace and healing love of Jesus Christ is stronger and can vanquish all evil, all despair, all darkness." This is not repressing your feelings, Paul, this is God's light filling all the darkness in you, and driving out what is not of Him. And in the space you have been moving into spiritually, psychology is not enough—spirit must be fought with Spirit. Don't let yourself be convinced that your patterns cannot be changed; or let yourself be drained—this is war! I am praying for you.

A catharsis of all the hurt, rejection, self-doubt I have ever experienced in my life—all piled into these few days. A bringing to consciousnesss (light) a whole part of me that I have suppressed. . .I have often longed to cry to get some release of pent-up hurts and could not.

A clearer and clearer invitation from God to be my Father and Lover, healing all these hurts and being above sufficient.

Later:

When I went outside at eleven, the world was new. Everything a revelation of God. Immense joy. I laughed aloud.

Walked in the fields singing and poeticizing to my heart's content, like a little boy set free to wander under the gaze of a loving Father.

*Hymn of the Universe**

Meanwhile my gaze had come to rest without conscious intention on a picture representing Christ offering his heart to men. The picture was hanging in front of me on the wall of a church into which I had gone to pray. So, pursuing my train of thought, I began to ask myself how an artist could contrive to represent the holy humanity of Jesus without imposing on his body a fixity, a too precise definition, which would seem to isolate him from all other men, and without giving to his face a too individual expression so that, while being beautiful, its beauty would be of a particular kind, excluding all other kinds.

It was then, as I was keenly pondering over these things and look-ing at the picture, that my vision began. To tell the truth, I cannot say at what precise moment it began, for it had already reached a certain degree of intensity when I became conscious of it. The fact remains that as I allowed my gaze to wander over the figure's outlines, I suddenly became aware that these were melting away: they were dissolving, but in a special manner, hard to describe in words. When I tried to hold in my gaze the outline of the figure of Christ it seemed to me to be clearly defined; but then, if I let this effort relax, at once these contours, and the folds of Christ's garment, the luster of his hair and the bloom of his flesh, all seemed to merge as it were (though without vanishing away) into the rest of the picture. It was as though the planes which marked

112

off the figure of Christ from the world surrounding it were melting into a single vibrant surface whereon all demarcations vanished.

It seems to me that this transformation began at one particular point on the outer edge of the figure; and that it flowed on thence until it had affected its entire outline. This at last is how the process appeared to me to be taking place. From this initial moment, moreover, the metamorphosis spread rapidly until it had affected everything.

First of all I perceived that the vibrant atmosphere which surrounded Christ like an aureole was no longer confined to a narrow space about him, but radiated outwards to infinity. Through this there passed from time to time what seemed like trails of phosphorescence, indicating a continuous gushing-forth to the outermost spheres of the realm of matter and delineating a sort of blood stream or nervous system running through the totality of life.

The entire universe was vibrant! And yet, when I directed my gaze to particular objects, one by one, I found them still as clearly defined as ever in their undiminished individuality.

All this movement seemed to emanate from Christ, and above all from his heart. And it was while I was attempting to trace the emanation to its source and to capture its rhythm that, as my attention returned to the portrait itself, I saw the vision mount rapidly to its climax.

I notice I have forgotten to tell you about Christ's garments. They had that luminosity we read of in the account of the Transfiguration; but what struck me most of all was the fact that no weaver's hand had fashioned them—unless the hands of angels are those of Nature. No coarsely spun threads composed their weft; rather it was matter, a bloom of matter, which had spontaneously woven a marvellous stuff out of the inmost depths of its substance; and it seemed as though I could see the stitches running on and on indefinitely, and harmoniously blending together in to a natural design which profoundly affected them in their own nature.

But, as you will understand, I could spare only a passing glance for this garment so marvellously woven by the continuous cooperation of all the energies and the whole order of matter: it was the transfigured face of the Master that drew and held captive my entire attention.

You have often at night-time seen how certain stars change their color from the gleam of blood-red pearls to the luster of violet velvet. You have seen, too, the play of colors on a transparent bubble. So it was that on the unchanging face of Jesus there shone, in an indescribable shimmer or iridescence, all the radiant hues of all our modes of beauty. I cannot say whether this took place in answer to my desires or in obedience to the good pleasure of him who knew and directed my desires; what is certain is that these innumerable gradations of majesty, of sweetness, of irresistible appeal, following one another or becoming transformed and melting into one another, together made up a harmony which brought me complete satiety.

And always, beneath this moving surface, upholding it and at the same time gathering it into a higher unity, there hovered the incommunicable beauty of Christ himself. Yet that beauty was something I divined rather than perceived; for whenever I tried to pierce through the covering of inferior beauties which hid it from me, at once other individual and fragmentary beauties rose up before me and formed another veil over the true Beauty even while kindling my desire for it and giving me a foretaste of it.

It was the whole face that shone in this way. But the center of the radiance and the iridescence was hidden in the transfigured portrait's eyes.

Over the glorious depths of those eyes there passed in rainbow hues the reflection—unless indeed it were the creative prototype, the Idea of everything that has power to charm us, everything that has life. . . . And the luminous simplicity of the fire which flashed from them changed, as I struggled to master it, into an inexhaustible complexity wherein were gathered all the glances that have ever warmed and mirrored back a human heart. Thus, for example, these eyes which at first were so gentle and filled with pity that I thought my mother stood before me, became an instant later like those of a woman, passionate and filled with the power to subdue, yet at the same time so imperiously pure that under their domination it would have been physically impossible for the emotions to go astray. And then they changed again, and became filled with a noble, virile majesty, similar to that which one sees in the eyes of men of great courage or refinement or strength, but incomparably more lofty to behold and more delightful to submit to.

This scintillation of diverse beauties was so complete, so captivating, and also so swift that I felt it touch and penetrate all my powers simultaneously, so that the very core of my being vibrated in response to it, sounding a unique note of expansion and happiness.

Now while I was ardently gazing deep into the pupils of Christ's eyes, which had become abysses of fiery, fascinating life, suddenly I beheld rising up from the depths of those same eyes what seemed like a cloud, blurring and blending all that variety I have been describing to you. Little by little an extraordinary expression, of great intensity, spread over the diverse shades of meaning which the divine eyes revealed, first of all permeating them and then finally absorbing them all . . . .

And I stood dumbfounded.

For this final expression, which had dominated and gathered up into itself all the others, was indecipherable. I simply could not tell whether it denoted an indescribable agony or a superabundance of triumphant joy. I only know that since that moment I thought I caught a glimpse of it once again—in the glance of a dying soldier.

In an instant my eyes were bedimmed with tears. And then, when I was once again able to look at it, the painting of Christ on the church wall has assumed once again its too precise definition and its fixity of feature.

* Teilhard de Chardin, *Hymn of the Universe*, Harper and Row, New York, 1965, used with permission.

Exercise in Awareness

The Father is constantly drawing us by the power of the Spirit to union with Him in Jesus.

"No one comes to Me unless the Father who sent Me draw Him" (Jn. 6:44).

How does the Father do this? How do we know about this activity? Through our experience as human beings.

We sense things with our eyes, ears, taste, smell, touch. We reflect upon what we see, hear, taste, smell, touch. We use our intellect to understand what we have sensed. We talk with others; we read; we remember. We experience the joy of intellectual insight and the desire to know more about God. But we also experience God through our heart, our affections, our feelings.

Feelings, affections, and even intellectual insights often operate in an unreflective way. We often follow them without thinking of them and their significance in our relationship with God. Yet, it is often in this way that the Lord draws us most intimately to himself. It is important then to become aware of these interior activities in order to know who I really am and who the Lord intends me to be as He draws me to himself.

The goal of our life is union with God. We can attain to this union only if we listen to Him and respond to his constant invitations to draw nearer. We said earlier that He draws each of us in a unique way, that

He makes his presence known in the level of our being where these movements register. There is another side to this, however. Our sinful nature also registers at the same level. This leaves us with a problem: If I am in touch with myself at this level of my being, then I am conscious of these other feelings as well. Which ones are leading me to the Lord and which are not?

I have to sort them out.

The problem is especially acute in our feeling life. We may even find it hard to get in touch with our feelings. Perhaps our training almost urged us to the opposite—to pay no attention to our feelings.

It Is Important To Know How You Feel.

We are not talking here about superficial sentiments but about the movements at the core of our being—deep in our hearts where God has placed his word.

If we stay away from this area—our real selves—we will be missing much of what the Spirit is saying to us and we will not become our true selves, because it is from this level of our being that we make our decisions, that we discover our real relationship with God, our true identity.

We discern what has to be faced, interpreted, decided, acted upon, in the light of this identity.

There is a time in the life of each person when he or she has to face such basic questions as these: Is God real? Does Jesus, risen and alive, mean anything to me?

If this person can gather together all the strands of the faith experience he has had and then say: "Yes, He is real! I have experience to back it up!"—Then his faith becomes more mature and he has a clearer grasp of his identity and relationship with God.

The experience that gives this conviction is called a *core faith experience*—the experience that opens one up to God—that basic total surrender to God that we have all experienced.

This may not have been a dramatic thing; it could have been a moment of quiet conviction when for the first time in my life I consciously surrendered totally to God, perhaps in fear, because I didn't know where He was taking me, but finally in joy and peace, because I had somehow experienced in the depths of my being what it was to be at one with God, at home with God.

This experience now becomes the touchstone of my life—the experience against which I test all my other experiences to see if they square with that feeling of being "at home" with God.

If I take each present interior experience and drop it down inside myself at that level where I am still trying to live out my total surrender, my "Yes, Father," and if it fits into that stance before God, then this will be a sign to me that it is right and good and from God. There will be a sense of rightness, peace, and joy.

But if I take my present interior experience and test it against my core experience of God and all disturbance and anxiety, then I can suspect that God is not the source of these movements. I do not feel at home with God.

It is important for us to be in touch with our feelings, to sort them out, and not be controlled by them.

THE EXERCISE

One of the best instruments to keep me in touch with my true self is the awarness exercise. Faithfulness to the daily examen is extremely important. The daily examen has two aspects to it: the art of Christian living and the experience of such living. The art requires an examination of our own efforts, that is, how I have responded—my virtues and my faults as seen in my actions. The experience concerns an awareness of the interior movements we have been discussing. The examination in this part is one of the ways in which I have experienced God relating to me through these interior movements.

Often we have looked upon the daily examen as a time to examine ourselves on a particular or predominant fault or to see how we were growing in a particular virtue. This was not too bad, but it was certainly not all that St. Ignatius (from whom we inherit it) intended the daily examen to be. This was meant to be only a small part of the examen, but we made it the major or only part.

The emphasis here will be on the examining of our *experience* of the interior movements, indicating God's action in us.

Next to the Eucharist; this exercise can provide the occasion for the most intimate encounter of the day with Jesus. Its real goal is to help me keep the faith dimension in my life—to put me in touch with my real self before God. He is constantly drawing each of us to himself in an intimate and unique way.

If I live from day to day simply reacting spontaneously to all that comes to me, I may be failing to hear his gentle and quiet invitation, because there are two spontaneities at work in me: one, good, from God; the other, evil, and not from God.

The awareness exercise is to help me to respond to God's loving invitations, not just during the time of the exercise, but in all of my daily living. It is to help me be with God in everything.

It is primarily concerned not with good and bad actions, but with what occurs in us prior to action: our deep inner feelings; how we are experiencing the drawing of the Father; how our sinful nature is quietly tempting and luring us away from our Father in subtle dispositions within us.

It is an exercise in awareness—awareness of my present relationship with a loving Father whose invitations to draw nearer to him are presenting themselves in new forms at every moment. It is not possible for me to make this kind of exercise without confronting my own identity in Christ before the Father.

I am a person with vows of marriage or religion, living in community and having a certain apostolate. All this is part of my identity—*my second name of grace.* But more than this—over the years I have come to know God's special ways of drawing me and I am aware of my past responses and how my life has been shaped because of this. I answer to a name that no one else answers to—*my first name of grace.* Each day the Lord in inviting me to deepen this identity.

THE AWARENESS EXERCISE AND PRAYER

It is my prayer that God gradually reveal to me both himself and the mystery of his plan for all reality in Christ. It is in prayer that I experience his invitations and challenges to *me personally.* This is why this exercise is prayer and is related to my daily, personal, contemplative prayer. My prayer would be empty if I did not order my life to respond to him. It is the awareness exercise that helps me to sense and recognize those interior invitations of the Lord that guide and deepen this ordering. To be prayerful means to be with God in all things, not just in the time of formal prayer.

THE FORMAT OF THE EXERCISE (cf. Sp. Exx. [43])

We must keep in mind the goal of the exercise—to develop a heart with a discerning vision that will be operating not just for ten or fifteen minutes during the exercise but throughout our whole day. Let us recall the five steps of the daily examen and see how they intend to lead us to this goal:

1. Thanksgiving
2. Prayer for light
3. Examination
4. Contrition and sorrow
5. Resolution

1. THANKSGIVING

If I see this exercise as related to prayer, I will readily understand why it is good to begin the examen with thanksgiving. In my prayer life I have come to realize that I am poor. I possess nothing, not even myself. I come before God as one who has been gifted by Him. I owe Him everything. The deeper my faith becomes, the more truly I become aware of my utter poverty and the more I am struck by God's great goodness to me. This sense of thankfulness should become an attitude that abides with me and remains a part of my constant awareness. So I use this time of the exercise to bring gratitude into my conscious awareness so that I can learn to have an abiding consciousness of who God is and how good He is. Gradually I will experience what it is to believe that *all is gift* and this awareness alone can change my life.

As I engage this part of the exercise, I thank God for everything and *specifically* for his gifts in the part of the day just completed. Expressing my gratitude will help me to discover gifts from God I didn't realize had been given. This examination will help me gradually to take a praising, thankful stance to the Lord at all times.

2. PRAYER FOR THE LIGHT OF THE SPIRIT

No doubt I have made enough mistakes in life to realize that seeing clearly into spiritual matters is a gift from beyond me. Since God knows me fully and knows who I will be when I become all I am capable of becoming, it is clear that only He can give me the needed insights into my life. It is important, then, that I ask for his Spirit to give me a growing insight into the mystery which I am.

I pray to become more and more Spirit-directed, to become open to *all* the channels by which He speaks to me. I pray to know how He has directed me in the events of this morning, this day, and how I have responded. I pray to experience his gifts in the events of today—a new peace, love, kindness, gentleness, patience, joy, fidelity, and self-control. I pray to become aware of the signs that I am not responding to God's love—the old anxiety, jealousy, bad temper, restlessness, anger, resentment, disagreements, infidelity, etc. (see Gal. 5:16-25).

3. THE EXAMINATION

This is the part of the exercise that we are most familiar with. It consists in examining our experience and actions.

A. Experience

Our real concern here is faith, and what has been happening to us and in us since the last examination. So the questions I ask myself could be similar to the following:

1) Did I feel drawn by the Lord any time today through: a companion, an event, a good book, nature, etc.? To what was he drawing me?

2) What have I learned today about Him and his ways—in the ordinary occasion, in stray moments?

3) How did I meet Him in fears, joys, misunderstanding, work, suffering?

4) How did his word come alive in me today—in my prayer time, in the Scriptures and other readings, in the liturgy?

5) In what ways have I encountered Christ through the members of my community? How have I brought Christ to them?

6) In what ways have I been the sign of God's presence and love—to

my companions, my friends, to the people I've met today?

7) Have I felt moved to go out of myself in concern for the lonely, sad, discouraged, needy?

8) How am I becoming more and more conscious of God's work—in the larger Church, in my country, in other countries of the world?

9) Have I experienced a growing awareness of: my being loved, my sinfulness, a desire to reciprocate, my dependence?

10) In what area of my being is Jesus not yet Lord?

B. Art

Secondly, we are concerned about the art of living, that is, our actions, insofar as they are responses to his calling. Too often we are so concerned with action that we become self-moved and motivated rather than moved and motivated by the Spirit. It is likely that the Lord is calling me to *conversion* in some area of my life. This is what I should be responding to instead of being busy in the area I choose to work on. Only God can reveal my sinfulness to me and He does so only out of love. So I examine how I have disposed myself for his call and how I have responded.

4. CONTRITION AND SORROW

A growing awareness of my sinfulness (my lack of response to love) will arouse in me:

Sorrow and wonder at being constantly brought to newness.

A sense of deep joy and gratitude because I have been guaranteed the victory through Christ.

A growing mistrust of self and firm trust in God.

A humble awareness of my weakness.

Here I can express sorrow over specific actions that were inadequate responses to his love at work in my heart.

5. HOPEFUL RESOLUTION FOR THE FUTURE

What I do in this part of the exercise should flow naturally from all that has preceded. Therefore, it will be different each day. If it were the same, it would be a sure sign that I have not really entered into the previous four elements of the exercise.

How do I look towards the future? Am I despondent, discouraged, fearful, hopeful, grateful, etc.? If so, why? I must be honest and not repress my true feelings.

With renewed vision and sensitivity I pray to *recognize* the ways in which the Lord calls me in each situation of the future, to *respond* to his call with more faith, humility, and courage, especially as I experience him calling for painful conversion in some areas of my heart.

I ask to be filled with hope, founded not on my own deserts or powers but in our Father, whose glorious victory in Jesus Christ I share through the life of their Spirit in my heart.

The more I trust God and allow Him to lead my life, the more I will experience true supernatural hope in Him, in and through Him, but beyond my weakness, pain, and poverty. And this experience brings joy!

"I leave the past behind and with hands outstretched to whatever lies ahead, I go straight for the goal" (Phil. 3:13).

Checklist of Blocks to Spiritual Awareness and Practice

No problems at all
Can't find the time
Other, more important things
Fear of losing control
Too tired usually
Can't concentrate
Feel tense, worried, afraid
Experience bad feelings/images
Sleep during prayer/meditation
Embarrassment, self-consciousness
Not comfortable physically
Not comfortable mentally
Can't stop thinking
Fear of Evil, the occult
Need to be logical, to understand
Bad feelings about myself
Fear of losing touch with myself
Can't give up my own will or need to control things
Fear of being tricked/fooled
Fear of death
Anger at Church, God, religion

Fear of God's judgment
Fear of God's demands
Fear that God won't be there
Bad feelings about others
Fear of using religion as an escape
Need to be *doing* something/can't just sit still
Get physical symptoms
Children, family demands
Feel selfish
Disbelief that God is a "person" to be talked to or listened to
Overfascination with certain experiences/can't get beyond them
Fear of losing friends
Fear of something nameless
Fear I won't be able to conceive
Fear I'll have to give up anger
Need for confession
Impatience
Can't think of words to pray
Afraid of failure
Don't know what I want
Spiritual feelings slip away
Feel no spiritual needs
Fear of feeling "holier than thou"
Get bored/restless
Don't trust spiritual leaders
Fear of changing personality
Fear of changing values
Fear of going crazy
Fear of fanaticism
It's too much work
Never get any results
Can't "just be"
Bad mood afterwards
Too much on my mind
Fear of getting too emotional
Fear of giving up other things
Scary experiences
Fear of losing faith

Fear of evangelism
Rebellion against the "shoulds" and "oughts" of religion
Haven't really been trying
Belief that man cannot help himself spiritually. . .only God can
Too many distractions
Feeling lonely, no support from others
Don't know how to do it
Guilt or shame
Can't discipline self
Pride gets in way of admitting any spiritual awareness needs
Fear of being changed
Rebellion against religious language
Fear of being ridiculed
Fear I'll lose sex appeal
Fear I'll cry publicly
Need to forgive someone/others
Need for God's forgiveness first

Prayer Questionnaire

1. Where and when do I pray?
2. What happens when I pray?
3. How long do I pray?
4. What kind of prayer do I use most?
5. To whom do I pray?
6. Why do I pray?
7. What do I want from my prayer?
8. How does prayer fit into my life?
9. How does my life fit into my prayer?
10. How do I evaluate my prayer?

Linda Sabbath's Role As Spiritual Director at the Center

By Barbara Rogers

Spiritual Direction does not necessarily presuppose the director's knowledge of the depths of the soul he reaches, or the full meaning of the words he pronounces. The efficacy of direction comes from God himself and need not be perceived by the speaker to do its work.

St. John of the Cross teaches: "These directors should reflect that they themselves are not the chief agent, guide and mover of souls in this matter, but that the principal guide is the Holy Spirit, who is never neglectful of souls, and that they are the instruments for directing them to perfection through faith and the law of God, according to the spirit God gives each one." His role is not the same as that of the teacher of the human sciences. A professor is appointed to teach philosophy, literature, and mathematics, which reveal only the conclusions of reason. It does happen that a director has greater experience and knowledge of spiritual traditions. He can, for instance, discern the sinful from the merely weak, or choose a modification best suited to his director's need and strength.

This "horizontal direction" is useful, and often bears fruit, but it is not sufficient in itself. We just join to it vertical direction, which takes into considerationt the grace proper to the one being directed. A delicate work! Even supposing that the continual advancements of psychology permits us to delve more deeply into the mystery of the individual, a sphere still remains that will escape scientific explanation. The director will never penetrate that sphere except with the light that God alone can dispense.

The job of the director does not stop at deep understanding of the one he is directing. His words must be efficacious; they must carry light and force. Only if the director is nothing but God's instrument will his word have the necessary power to convince and change.

This presence and this invisible action of God which St. Teresa of Avila experienced when she took counsel explains her attitude toward direction. When she was sick, her novices said to her: "Give us some advice about spiritual direction. How must we go about it?" She replied, "With great simplicity, but without relying too much on help which might prove inadequate when you come to make use of it . . . more often than not, you will find Jesus only after you have left all creatures behind." These counsels are nothing but the outcome of her own experience. She expressed he own conduct with regard to Father Pichon, enunciating a principle which modern psychology has confirmed. The gift of yourself to God will not be entire until you advance beyond the director, without ceasing to be directed.

As a priest said to St. Therese of Lisieux when she asked him to direct her: "My child, may Our Lord always be your superior and novice master." When she recalled this statement seven years later, she said: "He was this, in fact, and He was also my director. . . it was He who taught me that science hidden from the wise and the prudent and revealed to little ones" [*Correspondence*, p. 150.] In short, a good director is a blessing which you should seek like the pearl of great price, but if he or she does not appear, don't give up. Every one of us is only a prayer's reach away from St. Therese's Director of Directors.

In our own day, when we have learned so much about the twists and turns of the psyche, we are far more able to sort out our own delusions and rationalizations than were uneducated people of the Middle Ages. As Jacob Needleman wrote, "I take the aim of spiritual psychology to be the directing of our attention to what is really the case in ourself, free from egotistic reactions. . . ." [*Lost Christianity*, p. 49.] That attention is the overflow of contemplative prayer; it is a laser beam directed at the place in the soul that doesn't reflect God faithfully. If you have "seen God," you will also see where you fail to be his image. Having said this, however, let us remember our tendency to pride, sloth, and distortion of truth. Because, as modern physicists tell us, we are *incapable* of seeing reality objectively, we would do well "always and everywhere" to check out our self-perceptions for accuracy. If no trained director is available, you can look for a wise, prayerful friend, ideally much older and more experienced than you are, to advise you regularly. Or you can work with a small prayer group that knows you well and in whose members you have confidence. Above all, find someone who will tell you the truth about yourself, and learn from him or her to be honest in the face of God.

Bibliography

Berdyaev, Nikolai. *Slavery and Freedom*. New York: Charles Scribner and Sons, 1944.

Bouyer, Louis. *The Spirituality of the New Testament and the Fathers*. New York: The Seabury Press, 1963.

Brother Lawrence. *The Practice of the Presence of God*. Pyramid Publications, 1977.

Brown, Raymond E. *The Jerome Biblical Commentary*. Englewood Cliffs, N.J.: Prentice-Hall, Inc., 1968.

Buber, Martin. *Ten Rungs—Hasidic Sayings*. New York: Schocken Books, 1962.

De Chardin, Pierre Teilhard. *Hymn of the Universe*. London: William Collins Sons, 1965.

Ginn, Roman, OCSO. *Jonah—The Spirituality of a Runaway Prophet*. New York: Living Flame Press, 1978.

Jacobs, Louis. *Hasidic Thought*. New York: Schocken Books, 1972.

Kavanaugh, Kieran, OCD and Rodriguez, Otilio, OCD. *The Collected Works of St. John of the Cross* and *The Collected Works of St. Teresa of Avila*. ICS Publications, 1976 and 1979.

Keating, Thomas. *Open Mind, Open Heart*. Amity, N.Y.: Amity House, 1985.

Lossky, Vladimir. *The Vision of God*. The Faith Press, 1973.

———— . *In the Image and Likeness of God*. Crestwood, N.Y.: St. Vladimir's Seminary Press, 1974.

May, Gerald, M.D. *Care of Mind, Care of Spirit*. San Francisco: Harper & Row, 1982.

———— . *Will and Spirit*. New York: Harper & Row, 1982.

Miles, Margaret R. *Fullness of Life*. Philadelphia: The Westminster Press, 1981.

McEvoy, Hubert, SJ. *Work and Worship*. London: Burns and Oates Ltd., 1964.

P. Marie-Eugene, OCD. *I Want To See God*. Christian Classics, 1953.

Needleman, Jacob. *Lost Christianity*. New York: Bantam Books, 1980.

Otto, Rudolf. *The Idea of the Holy*. New York: Oxford University Press, 1958.

Pentecost, J. Dwight. *The Glory of God*. Multnomah Press, 1978.

Robb, Paul V., SJ. *Studies in the Spirituality of Jesuits*. American Assistancy Seminar on Jesuit Spirituality, USA, 1982.

Scholem, Gershom G. *Major Trends in Jewish Mysticism*. New York: Schocken Books, 1965.

———— . *On the Kabbalah and its Symbolism*. New York: Schocken Books, 1969.

Scupoli, Lorenzo. *Unseen Warfare*. Crestwood, N.Y.: St. Vladimir's Seminary Press, 1978.

Wojtyla, Karol. *Faith According to St. John of the Cross*. San Francisco: Ignatius Press, 1981.